Muslim Youth in NYC Public Schools Study

THIS IS WHERE I NEED TO BE
Oral Histories of Muslim Youth in NYC

Curriculum Guide & Reproducible Materials
A Resource for Teachers

created by Muslim Youth in NYC Public Schools Study & The Student Press Initiative

Copyright 2008
Student Press Initiative
Teachers College, Columbia University

ISBN: 978-1-932948-66-0

"A Lesson from Santa" by Cynthia Duxbury, Teaching Tolerance, Southern Poverty Law Center. Reprinted with permission of Teaching Tolerance and the Southern Poverty Law Center.

Curriculum Developer/Writer: Sandhya Nankani

Editor: Kerry McKibbin

Director, Muslim Youth In NYC Public Schools Study: Dr. Louis Cristillo

Curriculum Consultants: Uzma Akhand, Naazish YarKhan

Director of Programs, Student Press Initiative: Kerry McKibbin

Director of Production/Layout and Design: Jim Fenner

Founding Director, Student Press Initiative: Erick Gordon

Table of Contents

Introduction 5

5 Reasons to Teach This Book
by Dr. Louis Cristillo 7

Meet the Oral Historians 9

LESSONS

Is All Press Positive?: Analyzing Media and Propaganda about
Muslims in Post 9/11 America 15

Unity in Diversity: Exploring Islam in the United States 21

Don't Judge Me: Understanding the Power of a Stereotype 27

The ID Project: Exploring Identity Through the Lens of Culture and Religion 33

Choices, Choices: Considering the Pros and Cons of Peer Pressure 39

REPRODUCIBLES

Tabs on the Media 47

Wall of Fame: Personalities 49

Wall of Fame: Research Notes 51

Wall of Fame: Profile 53

A Lesson from Santa 55

Identity Chart 57

APPENDICES

Say It Out Loud: An Oral History Primer for Educators 59

Go Deeper: Additional Resources 67

INTRODUCTION

About one in ten students in New York City's public schools are Muslim—nearly 100,000 in all—yet they remain one of the most misunderstood segments of the student population. *This is Where I Need to Be* is a groundbreaking collection of oral history narratives from the lives of ordinary Muslim youth as told by Muslim youth. Published by the Student Press Initiative in 2008, it was a project that grew out of the *Muslim Youth in NYC Public Schools Study* directed by Dr. Louis Cristillo, Research Assistant Professor at Teachers College, Columbia University.

Introduced to the methods of oral history by a team of collaborating teachers at Teachers College, a dozen Muslim teenagers set out to document the real-life experiences and feelings of their Muslim peers in New York City high schools. The result is a compelling collection of twenty-three oral histories. These are voices of teenagers living ordinary lives at a time when being Muslim in America can provoke "extraordinary" reactions from classmates and teachers, from friends and strangers, and even from one's own family and kin. Whatever you think you know about Muslims in America, these stories rise above news-cycle stereotypes and open a personal window onto what it means to be young and Muslim.

This curriculum guide will help you bring the themes explored in these oral histories to life in your classroom. The guide features five lesson plans and companion reproducibles which can be taught over the course of one or two sessions, a semester or an entire year. Each lesson plan addresses the academic standards drawn from the Mid-Continent Research for Education and Learning's "Content Knowledge: A Compendium of Standards and Benchmarks for K-12 Education: 3rd and 4th Editions." In the appendices, you will find a comprehensive list of print, web, and literary resources, as well as an overview of oral history with suggestions on how to incorporate this form of storytelling and historical research into your teaching.

Rather than imposing a rigid age or grade structure on these materials, we have designed this curriculum guide to accommodate a wide range of student interests and capabilities. We encourage you to adapt the materials according to the needs, interests, and capabilities of your classes. After all, no one knows your students better than you do.

We look forward to receiving your feedback on these lessons and suggested activities. Please feel free to contact us at **publishspi@gmail.com** or through our website at www.publishspi.com.

Sandhya Nankani
Curriculum Guide Developer/Writer

5 Reasons to Teach This Is Where I Need To Be

By Dr. Louis Cristillo, Director
*Muslim Youth in NYC Public Schools Study and Research Assistant
and Professor at Teachers College, Columbia University*

1. It sheds light on a growing demographic that has been frequently misrepresented in post- 9/11 America.

Islam is one of the fastest growing religions in the United States and Muslim students are increasingly visible in classrooms. Muslim children come in all colors, races, ethnicities, and nationalities; some are religious while others are not. Yet, widespread Islamophobia in the wake of 9/11 makes many Muslim youth feel marginalized from the mainstream.

This is Where I Need to Be personalizes the experience of being Muslim and shows the diversity of its representation among youth from a cross-section of New York City's ethnic communities. It allows youth to speak for themselves and to represent their religiosity in discourse that is unfiltered by the news media, movies, and prejudices inherited from history and contemporary political propaganda. At the same time, it demonstrates that just as race, ethnicity, sexual orientation, and class can be anchors of identity, religion too can be a salient marker of identity for children and young adults.

2. It promotes tolerance in multicultural classrooms.

Despite the season of hope heralded by the election of Barack Obama, there are still entrenched suspicions and profound misconceptions about Islam and Muslim culture. It is important to seize the momentum of a new era of tolerance as an unparalleled opportunity to correct the enduring fears and misperceptions that feed into Islamophobia.

Educators need to recognize that Muslim youth are a growing segment of the public school enrollment in the United States. Children of immigrants who arrived in the 1970s and 1980s are now adults, and they are starting families—the second generation. These American Muslims and their children—the emerging third generation—are more connected to American culture, society and values than their immigrant parents and grandparents. Educators thus are in a privileged position to weave American Muslim youth into the fabric of their multicultural classrooms.

This book gives needed attention to the fact that Muslims are very much a part of the fabric of American religious diversity. It is a contribution toward dispelling many of the essentializing stereotypes that continue to cast Islam as one of the most misunderstood world religions in modern history.

3. It reflects the diversity and varied experiences of Muslim youth in the United States.

The Muslim community in New York City is a microcosm of the diversity of the Muslim population throughout the United States. Virtually every variety of immigrant group is represented be it South Asian, Arab, African, Southeast Asian or Eastern European, not to mention indigenous American Muslims of African American, Latino and white European ancestry.

The stories in *This is Where I Need to Be* grow from the experiences and perspectives of youth in public high schools. These are the lives of youth who represent a cross-section of the diversity of American Muslims in the United States. The stories reflect the variety of urban school environments in the U.S.: large and small, selective and regular, and all very diverse. Thus, any student who reads these stories, whether Muslim or not, will recognize something familiar while at the same time discovering something new.

4. It offers multidisciplinary teaching opportunities for the busy instructor.

This guide provides ready-made and adaptable lesson plans that are augmented with supplementary resources. It is a valuable didactic device that is intended to open opportunities and possibilities for all readers, young and old, and from all backgrounds to critically explore, discover, and interpret what is particular, universal and ordinary, and extraordinary in the lives, feelings, attitudes, experiences, aspirations and frustrations of Muslim American youth. It will help reduce any apprehensions that the average teacher may have in tackling content, themes or topics about which they may have little or incomplete knowledge.

Even though the book represents a specific literary genre—oral history—the curriculum guide provides a rich variety of content, ideas, activities, and supplementary resources that makes the book suitable not only for language arts, but also for arts and humanities, social studies, and American history.

5. It invites students to engage with oral history.

Reading oral history and doing oral history are transformative experiences. Oral history can stimulate critical reflection and curiosity and even lead to a profound understanding of people, places, times and events that conventional historiography usually trivializes.

Oral history creates narratives that recount ordinary lives of people who would otherwise never make it into history books, let alone have the opportunity to speak for themselves. It gives the reader an intimate connection to someone they might otherwise never get to know: the person they silently sit next to on a subway train or nonchalantly pass in the school hallway. In the words of Studs Terkel, oral history allows "people to talk to one another no matter what their difference of opinion might be." *

---

* From *Hope Dies Last: Making a Difference in an Indifferent World* (Granta Books, 2005) by Studs Terkel. Also excerpted in *The Life of Meaning: Reflections on Faith, Doubt, and Repairing the World* (Seven Stories Press, 2008) by Bob Abernethy, William Bole and Tom Brokaw.

Meet the Oral Historians

The stories in *This is Where I Need to Be* were collected and compiled by the following high school oral historians:

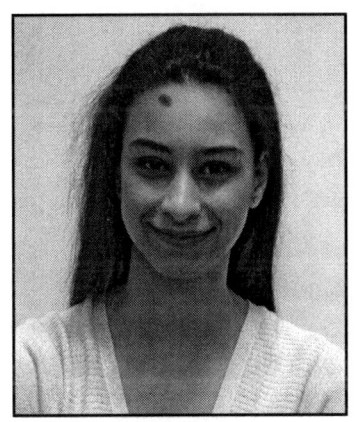

AMNA AHMAD is a seventeen-year-old Arab American of Palestinian ancestry in the 11th grade at a high school in Manhattan.

"While I am a Muslim student myself, the stories we gathered at the culmination of this project reveal to me for the first time a certain degree of boundlessness among Muslim youth as they search for their Islamic identities in the United States."

OMAR AHMAD is a fifteen-year-old Arab American of Palestinian ancestry in the 10th grade at a high school in Manhattan.

"I fully embraced this opportunity to give voice to a group of individuals whose views and lives are often misunderstood and neglected by many in America today—Muslim youth."

RAHIMAH AHMAD is a sixteen-year-old African American student in the 10th grade at a high school in Manhattan.

"During the interview process… I realized that it's not just people who aren't Muslim who assume things about Muslims. We Muslims do this, too. I really hope this book will demolish many of the common assumptions people make about Muslims—for Muslims and non-Muslims alike."

ATEEYAH KHAN is a seventeen-year-old Guyanese-born American student in the 12th grade at a high school in Queens.

"As I sat down to put these stories together I realized that so many of us go through the same discrimination, but never had the chance to express ourselves and our emotions. Every story I read or wrote made an impact in my life. Outsiders can relate with the struggle the Muslim youth go through in New York City and that there is no difference between race, sex, and religion."

SADIA KHAN is a sixteen-year-old South Asian American student of Pakistani ancestry in the 11th grade at a high school in Queens.

"Many Muslims are intimidated to speak out and express their ideas for fear of being persecuted in grocery stores, schools, malls, or of even being detained and sent to jail. I hope we can bring change with this book and impact people's lives. I would like it to change the vilification of Muslims… I want the world to be a peaceful place, not just for Muslims, but for every person who follows a religion."

FAATIMAH KNIGHT is a sixteen-year-old Caribbean American student in the 10th grade at a high school in Brooklyn.

"The interview helped me level two important aspects of my life: my religion and individuality, two things that at times may seem in opposition to each other. It felt reassuring to talk to a Muslim who, like myself, struggles to harmonize religion and New York City where the lights are bright and the temptations easily satisfied."

ABDULLA MOHAMED is a sixteen-year-old Arab American student born in Yemen who is in the 11th grade at a high school in the Bronx.

"Being part of this book is one of the biggest turning points of my life. I hope with this book Muslims will be treated equally and not be recognized as different people."

MURTAZA MUNIR is an eighteen-year-old South Asian American student of Pakistani ancestry born in Kuwait. He is in the 12th grade at a high school in Brooklyn.

"Last year around the same time period I was just a regular student in an urban high school in Brooklyn, but today I am an oral historian as well as a published author. As I sat down to put these stories together, it came to my attention that I have been through some similar situations at some points in my life."

KENAN SHABIU is an eighteen-year-old American student born in Kosovo. He is in the 12th grade at a high school in the Bronx.

"This project can help everyone know more about the lives of Muslim students in schools. It also shows to other people how Muslim students and their families are a part of this city. By sharing the work that we did, this might change the views of people all over the world about Muslims in America."

HUSEIN YATABARRY is a fifteen-year-old Gambian American student in the 10th grade at a high school in the Bronx.

"There are opportunities that you get in life that are very rare. If you happen to pass them up, you'll regret it. This project was one of those opportunities. It shed light on common misconceptions people have about Muslims and provided us with an opportunity to challenge them. The stories of Muslim youth will be part of history and will inform people about the lives of youth who are often not heard in our society."

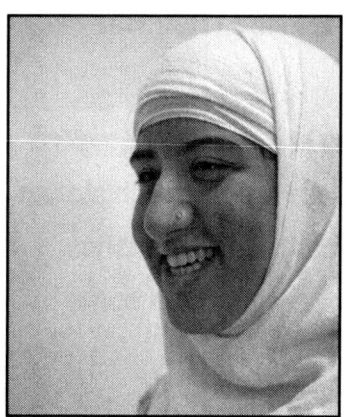

QUAINAT ZAMAN is a fifteen-year-old South Asian American student of Pakistani ancestry in the 10th grade at a high school in Staten Island.

"Something surprising about the project was that I was able to relate to both of my interviewees. I was able to relate with Fanta when she said she does track. Her event is hurdles. I do track, too, and a hurdle is the perfect symbol of the obstacles that we face as young Muslim women.... Before the project, I felt like I was one of the only Muslims to struggle with temptations, but afterwards I realized that I'm not."

HODA ZAWAM is a seventeen-year-old Arab American student born in Egypt who is in the 11th grade in Brooklyn.

"My fellow oral historians and I are pleased to share with you, the reader, the real lives and experiences and authentic voices of ordinary Muslim public school students. These stories give a shout out to all the Muslims in public school by telling them to stay strong, continue to believe, and always be proud to be a Muslim."

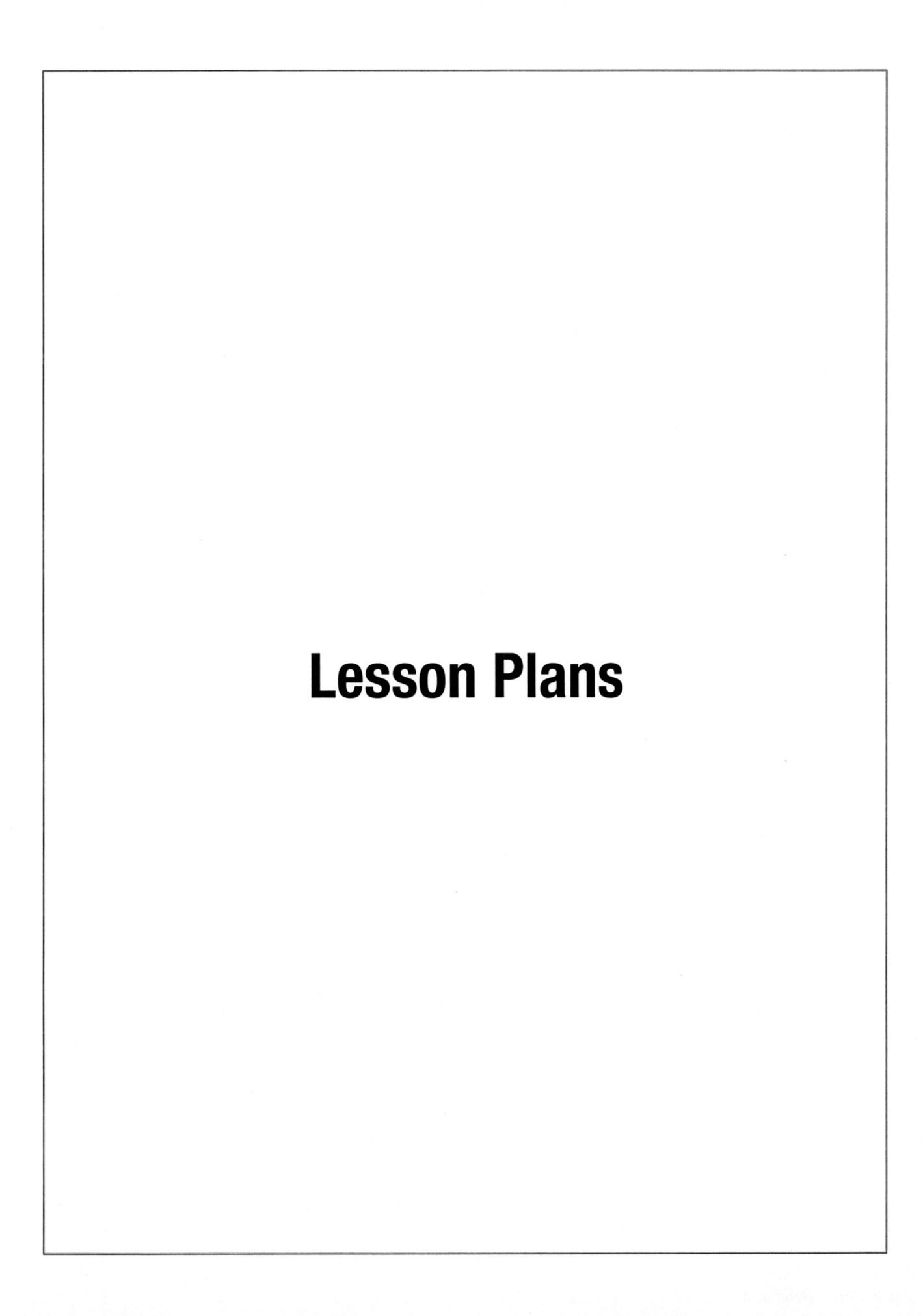

Lesson Plans

Lesson Plan: Is All Press Positive?

Analyzing Media Bias in Post 9/11 America

Overview

In this lesson, students will examine and evaluate the role of the media in depicting Muslims and Islam in post-9/11 America by comparing oral history perspectives and examples from current media.

Procedure

1. Warm-up/Conversation Starters

The following questions were asked in a 2006 Washington Post poll:

a. Do you feel you do or do not have a good basic understanding of the teachings and beliefs of Islam, the Muslim religion?

b. Would you say you have a generally favorable or unfavorable opinion of Islam?

c. Every religion has mainstream beliefs, and also fringe elements or extremists. Thinking of mainstream Islam, do you think mainstream Islam teaches respect for the beliefs of non-Muslims, or not?

d. Do you think mainstream Islam encourages violence against non-Muslims, or is it a peaceful religion?

e. Compared to other religions, do you think there are more violent extremists within Islam, fewer, or about the same number as in other religions?

f. Have you recently heard other people say prejudiced things against Muslims, or not? IF YES: Have you heard that kind of thing a lot, or not much?

g. Do you have any close friends or relatives who you'd describe as prejudiced against Muslims, or not?

Grades
6-12

Subjects
- Civics
- Current Events
- Language Arts
- Media Studies

Materials Needed

a. *This Is Where I Need to Be*— Chapters 4, 7, 8, 9, 13, and 16 connect most strongly to this lesson.

b. Old issues of news magazines such as Time, Newsweek, US News and World Report and/or newspapers.

c. Reproducible: "Tabs on the Media" on page 51.

Key Terms

stereotypes, media bias, Islamophobia, 9/11, Islam, Muslim, propaganda

According to the 2006 Washington Post poll where these questions were posed,

46% of Americans have a negative view of Islam.

This view has been sharpened since the attacks of 9/11.

Prompt your students to answer the questions asked in the 2006 Washington Post poll with one of the following responses: (a) Yes (b) No (c) No opinion. You may choose to conduct the poll by having students raise their hands in response and by keeping track of their responses on the board, or by asking students to answer the questions on a separate piece of paper and tallying their responses.

Share the results of the poll with students.

Ask: Why do you think this might be the case?
Tell them how their responses measure up against this national poll.

Ask students to reflect on the possible sources of the public's negative perceptions about Islam:

- Are they fact-based?

- Are they based on something they saw in the news, in a film, or on television?

- Are they based on current events?

- Or, are they based on something that a loved or trusted person has told them?

Use this conversation to get students thinking and talking about the connection between perceptions and the representation of Islam and Muslims in the media since 9/11.

2. Questions for Class Discussion

As a class, read and discuss the related chapters in *This is Where I Need to Be*, focusing on the following:

a. Make a list of the words and "stereotypes" that the authors of these oral histories feel are repeatedly used to describe them. What event, in their opinion, spurred such depictions?

b. What symbol of peace is "stripped of its intended meaning," according to Adam? Why might this be so upsetting to him?

c. On page 48, Sabeen Sheikh expresses her frustration with "the news." What is it about the news that bothers her?

d. On page 59, Hagar Omran says that he thinks "that Muslims are not depicted correctly here in America, especially through the media." What is the effect of such depictions, according to him?

e. On page 15, Hussein talks about his dream of becoming an international journalist. What does he hope to accomplish through this dream?

3. Class Project

Share with students that they will be investigating the assertions, as read in the oral histories, that the media has been unfair in its depiction of Muslims and Islam.

Explain to students that they will be reviewing assorted print and online media for articles, speeches, or political cartoons featuring Muslims or Islam, keeping an eye out for positive or negative images, representations or biases. Divide them into small groups and provide each group with a selection of news magazines and/or newspaper articles that you have collected. If your class has Internet access, you may also wish to direct students to some of the websites listed in the "Related Resources" section below. Have students skim and scan these sources and use the reproducible "Tabs on the Media" on page 51 to record and analyze their findings.

When students have completed their assignment, reconvene as a large group to review their conclusions. To wrap up the activity, ask students to discuss their answers to the "So What?" question (found at the bottom of "Tabs on the Media") and to evaluate whether they better understand the perspectives of the authors of *This is Where I Need to Be.*

4. Homework & Assignments

a. Students watch and compare a single night's episode of BBC News (on PBS) and World News Tonight (on ABC), and take notes on the differences in terms of headlines, geographic coverage, visual images, and words used to describe Muslims or Islam (if any). They can use "Tabs on the Media" on page 51 for this assignment.

Related Resources

The following websites take an unfiltered look at media bias in post 9/11 America, offering examples and statistics that your students may find useful for the class project or longer-term assignments.

Muslim While Flying

Award-winning short video by Ali Ardekani, a video blogger, about stereotypes and media generalizations towards Muslims.
http://tinyurl.com/6lx9u8

Negative Perception of Islam Increasing

Washington Post article about Washington Post/ABC News 2006 survey results.
http://tinyurl.com/nff8b

Council on American Islamic Relations (CAIR)

The website of CAIR provides a thorough look at the rise of Islamophobia—unfounded fear or and hostility toward Islam—in the US post 9/11.
http://www.cair.com/Issues/Islamophobia/Islamophobia.aspx

Related Resources

FAIR Smearcasters
This 2008 report documents examples of Islamophobic references in the media. Compiled by the nonprofit "Fairness and Accuracy in Reporting."
http://www.smearcasting.com/

Obsession with Hate
This site created by the nonpartisan community coalition, Hate Hurts America, looks at the distribution of 28 million copies of the anti-Muslim DVD "Obsession" during the 2008 election campaign.
www.obsessionwithhate.com/

CNN's Campbell Brown "So What if Obama is a Muslim?"
CNN's Campbell Brown speaks out about media bias during the 2008 election campaign.
http://tinyurl.com/3o6dz5

Colin Powell on "Meet the Press"
During his appearance on NBC's "Meet the Press" during the 2008 Presidential campaign, former Secretary of State Gen. Colin Powell questions the bias against Barack Obama due to his middle name "Hussein" and asks, "Is there something wrong with being Muslim in this country? No, that's not America. Is there something wrong with some seven-year-old Muslim American kid believing that he or she could be president?"
http://tinyurl.com/59sang

b. Students research and analyze the representation of Muslims in the media since 9/11 by collecting editorial and political cartoons. Possible sources for research include cartoonstock.com and cagle.com. Students might create a classroom gallery and write a statement in response to the question: What are some typical misperceptions and stereotypes Westerners hold about Islam and the Middle East, and vice versa?

c. Students investigate the presence of an anti-Muslim bias in the election campaign of 2008. They collect quotes from politicians, public citizens, and journalists to develop a case study on election propaganda and public opinion.

d. Students research biases against minority groups over time. They create a timeline that connects major world or national events with an upsurge of violence or bias against a cultural, ethnic, or religious group.

5. Assessment

Teacher evaluation of classroom participation. Teachers may wish to develop additional rubrics and measures for class projects and longer-term assignments.

6. National Standards

These academic standards are drawn from the *Mid-Continent Research for Education and Learning's "Content Knowledge: A Compendium of Standards and Benchmarks for K-12 Education: 3rd and 4th Editions."*

Grades 6-8
- *Civics Standard 19:* Understands what is meant by "the public agenda," how it is set, and how it is influenced by public opinion and the media.
- *Geography Standard 13:* Understands the forces of cooperation and conflict that shape the divisions of Earth's surface.

- *Language Arts Standard 1:* Demonstrates competence in the general skills and strategies of the writing process.
- *Language Arts Standard 7:* Demonstrates competence in the general skills and strategies for reading a variety of informational texts.

Grades 9-12
- *Geography Standard 10:* Understands the nature and complexity of Earth's cultural mosaics.

Related Resources

Media Matters for America

The not-for-profit research and information center dedicated to monitoring, analyzing, and correcting misinformation in the U.S. media keeps track of media-based attacks on Muslims and Islam.
http://tinyurl.com/fgxob

Islamophobia Watch

A non-profit online project to document material in the public domain which advocates a fear and hatred of the Muslim peoples of the world and Islam as a religion.
www.islamophobia-watch.com/

Lesson Plan: **Unity in Diversity**

Exploring Islam in the United States

Overview

In this lesson, students will examine the cultural, geographic, and linguistic diversity of the Muslim community in America, developing an understanding of its historical roots and heterogeneous nature.

Procedure

1. Warm-up/Conversation Starters

Share the following with your students: Did you know?

- There are 5 to 7 million Muslims in the United States.
- They are African Americans, South Asians, Middle Easterners, Africans, Europeans, and many more.
- 64 percent of Arab Americans are Christian.
- The Christian Word for God in Arabic speaking nations is Allah.

Divide students into two groups and ask each group to find the answers to the following questions. Provide them with a copy of Change the Story's "A Timeline of Muslim Events in America":

a. Who were some of the first Muslim arrivals in America?

b. Where and when was the first American mosque built? By which ethnic group?

Reconvene the class and ask students to share their responses. Then, using a world map, have students pinpoint the countries that came up in their answers to the above questions. Ask them to identify other countries of the world where Muslims in the U.S. originate.

Grades
6-12

Subjects
- Civics
- American History
- Language Arts
- Media Studies
- Social Studies
- Global History

Materials Needed

a. *This Is Where I Need To be*—Chapters 1, 2, 6, and 19 connect most strongly to this lesson. Other related chapters are 7, 20, 22, and 23.

b. Copies of "A Timeline of Muslim Events in America" from Change the Story at http://tinyurl.com/5mbyqq

c. Reproducible—"Wall of Fame: Personalities" on page 53.

d. Reproducible—"Wall of Fame: Research Notes" on page 55.

e. Reproducible—"Wall of Fame: Profile" on page 57.

Key Terms

identity, multi-cultural, cultural diversity, mosques in America, Muslims in America, American History, slavery, African American Muslims, heritage, faith, Islam

Monolithic (adj.):

Characterized as a uniform whole, without any differences

Once the map activity is completed, if it hasn't already been identified, place a pin on the USA and remind students that many African American Muslims are able to trace their Islamic heritage to the Muslims who were brought to America as slaves from Africa.

Ask students to discuss the following questions:

- Did your findings surprise you? Why or why not?

- How do you think geographical and linguistic differences play a role in a person's religious identity?

- If Muslims in America come from such diverse backgrounds and nations, do you think there is such a thing as one **monolithic** Islamic culture?

Share with students that they are going to focus on gaining a better understanding of the heterogeneous nature of the Muslim community in the United States.

2. Questions for Class Discussion

As a class, read and discuss the related chapters in *This is Where I Need to Be*, focusing on the following:

a. Make a list of the phrases that the authors use to speak about their identities and the countries from which they originate. What stands out to you when you look at this list? How do you understand your readings in the context of the following quote from a letter Malcolm X, a black Civil Rights leader, wrote on his pilgrimage to Mecca:

> *During the past eleven days here in the Muslim world, I have eaten from the same plate, drunk from the same glass and slept in the same bed (or on the same rug) while praying to the same God with fellow Muslims, whose eyes were the bluest of the blue, whose hair was the blondest of blond, and whose skin was the whitest of white. And in the words and in the actions and in the deeds of the 'white' Muslims, I felt the same sincerity that I felt among the black African Muslims of Nigeria, Sudan and Ghana. We are truly all the same—brothers.*

b. What do you notice about the names of some of those authors featured in the oral histories: Priscilla, Danielle, Adam, Fanta, Sokol, Tania? What conclusions can you draw from these names about Muslims and their cultural backgrounds?

c. How do you understand these oral histories in the context of the following remark by Dr. Umar Abd-Allah, author of *A Muslim in Victorian America: The Story of Alexander Russell Webb*:

> For centuries, Islamic civilization harmonized indigenous forms of cultural expression with the universal norms of its sacred law. It…fanned a brilliant peacock's tail of unity in diversity from the heart of China to the shores of the Atlantic. …in that regard, (Islam) has been likened to a crystal clear river. Its waters (Islam) are pure, sweet, and life-giving but—having no color of their own—reflect the bedrock (indigenous culture) over which they flow. In China, Islam looked Chinese; in Mali, it looked African.

d. Find a passage in Chapter 1 where the author reflects on her relationship with a non-Muslim member of her family. What do we learn about the author's relationship with that family member and her extended family? Can you identify with this experience in some way? Give an example.

e. Based on these oral histories, analyze the connection between the authors' religion, cultural background, and identity. How do the three intersect? How did these oral histories make you think differently about your understanding of Muslims in America?

3. Class Project

On the reproducible **"Wall of Fame: Personalities"** on page 53 you will find a list of notable historical, literary, political, and cultural figures, all of whom happen to be Muslim. Separate the names, put them all into a hat and ask each student to pick one name. Tell students that they are going to be researching and writing mini-biographies to create a "Wall of Fame" which will highlight the Muslim community's diversity and contributions to society.

Have students use the handout **"Wall of Fame: Research Notes"** on page 55 to collect and compile their information. They can then consolidate their research, using the reproducible **"Wall of Fame: Profile"** on page 57.

Related Resources

The following materials offer more information on the Muslim community in the United States.

"A Muslim In Victorian America: The Life of Alexander Russell Webb," by Dr. Umar F. Abd-Allah

This biography (Oxford University Press, 2006) chronicles the life and times of journalist Alexander Russell Webb, contemporary of Mark Twain, and the first known Victorian American convert to Islam.

Prince Among Slaves

This PBS documentary traces the roots of Islam in America to the slave trade, and especially West Africa. The website also includes a teacher's guide.
http://tinyurl.com/526knt

Frontline: Portraits of Ordinary Muslims in America

PBS offers a look at ordinary Muslims in various parts of the world. This segment focuses on Muslims in America.
http://tinyurl.com/5tz7bl

A teacher's guide is also available at
http://tinyurl.com/5kyzd2

Related Resources

Change the Story
Resources at this educational website include "What is Islam?" and "Islam 101" as well as a downloadable PDF quiz, "The Millionaire Quiz" and a timeline of Islam.
http://changethestory.net/?q=content/resources-everybody

Reporting on Religion: A Primer for Journalists
Religion Newswriters provides a thorough introduction to Islam for religion journalists. This may also be helpful in the classroom.
http://www.rnasecure.org/guide/islam.html

Muslims, by Paul D. Numrich
This entry from the Encyclopedia of Chicago examines Chicago as a microcosm of the theological, ethnic and cultural diversity of Islam.
http://www.encyclopedia.chicagohistory.org/pages/865.html

U.S. Religious Landscape Survey
Based on interviews with more than 35,000 American adults, this extensive survey by the Pew Forum on Religion & Public Life details the religious makeup, religious beliefs and practices as well as social and political attitudes of the American public, including the Muslim community.
http://religions.pewforum.org/

If Internet access is available, students might also write their biographies following a wikipedia format and post them on a group blog, using blogger.com or a similar blogging site. To create a character sketch on their blog, students can:

- Write a short biography of the person they researched.
- Add quotes by or about them.
- add excerpts from and/or links to articles written by or about them.
- post images, art and lyrics to songs they feel express the personality of this individual.

When students are finished, you might have them do oral presentations about the individuals they researched. You may also create an exhibit highlighting their work.

Afterwards, reconvene the class and evaluate their experiences with this assignment. Some reflection questions you might pose are:

- What aspect(s) of their research did they find most fascinating?
- What aspect(s) did they find most surprising?
- Would they use what they now know to dispel myths and misinformation about Muslims on an individual as well as on a collective, large-scale basis? If yes, how?

4. Homework & Assignments

a. Have students take Changethestory.net's "Millionaire Quiz" online at **http://tinyurl.com/5w5m8j.** It tests students' knowledge of Muslims on everything from demographic information to cultural and artistic contributions, and would provide an interesting launching pad for group discussions or further research.

b. Ask students to view the PBS documentary *Prince Among Slaves* which examines the roots of Islam in America. This PBS documentary tells the story of Abdul Rahman, an African Muslim prince. In 1788, the year Abdul Rahman was sold into slavery, his father controlled a country larger than the United States at the time. Yet, once captured and sold, Rahman would struggle and toil for 40 long years. Through it all, he strove to hold onto his Muslim identity.

Following the movie, divide students into small groups and have them discuss the following questions before reconvening and sharing their findings with the rest of the class:

1. Were you previously familiar with the fact that many of the slaves brought to America were Muslim? Does this movie change any prior perceptions you had, especially about African Americans today?
2. Were you surprised to learn that people of aristocracy were also amongst those enslaved? Why or why not?
3. What was there about the protagonist's sense of identity that empowered him to stay hopeful and determined? Illustrate with three examples from the movie.
4. Many slaves had to take on the names of their owners. In the context of identity, why do you feel the slave-owners practiced this?

   c. Ask students to answer/ the following questions:
- What religious food and drink restrictions do Muslims have?
- Do you have any foods that you can't eat for health or religious reasons?

Have students find two recipes reflecting the food prepared in any three Muslim countries or by Muslim families in the United States. You can culminate this research assignment by hosting a food festival where students bring in foods from different parts of the Muslim world, including the United States. Or, students can create a recipe book of "Muslim Foods" which shows the cultural diversity of the cuisines that are shared by members of one religion. This activity further reinforces the lesson that while the religious tenets of Islam are often one and the same, Islamic culture varies from region to region.

d. Students find photos and provide a brief description of wedding dresses worn by Muslim brides: one bride from the Middle East and one from South Asia. Ask students to compare the common features and the differences in both wedding dresses and wedding celebrations of either region, then extend their understanding to at least one other religion of the world.

e. Have students go online and find photos of the different mosques in the United States. Encourage them to explore whether all U.S. mosques are identical. They should note the salient features of three mosques in the U.S. or in New York City—including dominant architectural influences—and

Related Resources

"Mosque, Possibly Oldest in Bakersfield, Follows a Unique Path," by Louis Medina
The article from "The Bakersfield Californian" examines the Bakersfield Muslim Center in California, a storefront mosque with a largely African American congregation of converts to Islam.
http://www.bakersfield.com/138/story/570294.html

"A Crown Jewel", by Zerqa Abid
This article from Islamic Horizons magazine (see page 42) features the Noor Islamic Cultural Center in Central Ohio, a mosque built primarily by immigrant Muslims. Members of the congregation speak on how the mosque is a 'symbol' and an expression of their identities as Muslims in America.
http://tinyurl.com/5j9xsu

"The Dome and the Grid," by Jerrilynn D. Dodds
The diversity that is New York is reflected in its mosques. This article in Aramco World Magazine explores how architectural space has been used to create an identity for Muslims who represent such diverse cultures and languages. She explores how these buildings represent Islam as a distinct way of life and an integrated part of New York's secular landscape.
http://tinyurl.com/635ds4

Related Resources

"Don't Forget African American Muslims," by Dr. Aminah McCloud

In "Common Ground News," Dr. Aminah McCloud argues that African American Muslims, being part of the American ethos for centuries prior to the arrival of immigrant Muslims, are best positioned to bridge gaps between Muslims and America.
http://tinyurl.com/6pr3l9

"Black Slaves Brought Arabic literacy, Islamic faith to America," by Rachel Hamm

This article from North Texas Daily student newspaper reviews a talk given by Dr. Yushau Sodiq, Texas Christian University Religion Professor, that provides insights and dispels myths about African slaves.
http://tinyurl.com/598a6l

"Imam W. Deen Mohammed Dies at 74, His Embrace of Traditional Islam led to Rift with Nationalists," by Margaret Ramirez and Manya A. Brachear

This article from The Los Angeles Times looks at the single most important man in the African American Muslim community, Imam W. Deen Mohammed. It explores how he established his own identity, forgoing that of his father and the Nation of Islam and illustrates how one person can serve as a catalyst to reinvent, and redirect, a whole community, in this case African American Muslims of America.
http://tinyurl.com/6hls3g

list what makes each mosque unique and which features the mosques have in common. **Ask:**
- How do mosque features reflect cultural or ethnic variations among the Muslim community?
- What do they tell you about Muslims in the United States and their identity given the kinds of mosques you see built here?

5. Assessment

Teacher evaluation of classroom participation. Teachers may wish to develop additional rubrics and measures for class projects and longer-term assignments.

6. National Standards

These academic standards are drawn from the *Mid-Continent Research for Education and Learning's "Content Knowledge: A Compendium of Standards and Benchmarks for K-12 Education: 3rd and 4th Editions."*

Grades 6-12

- *Language Arts Standard 8:* Uses listening and speaking strategies for different purposes
- *Language Arts Standard 9:* Uses viewing skills and strategies to understand and interpret visual media.
- *Behavioral Studies Standard 1:* Understands that group and cultural influences contribute to human development, identity, and behavior
- *US History Standard 31:* Understands economic, social, and cultural developments in the contemporary United States
- *Civics Standard 11:* Understands the role of diversity in American life and the importance of shared values, political beliefs, and civic beliefs in an increasingly diverse American society
- *Civics Standard 23:* Understands the impact of significant political and nonpolitical developments on the United States and other nations
- *Art Connections Standard 1:* Understands connections among the various art forms and other disciplines
- *World History Standard 46:* Understands long-term changes and recurring patterns in world history

Lesson Plan: **Don't Judge Me**

Understanding the Power of a Stereotype

Overview

In this lesson, students will examine the origins and manifestations of negative stereotypes in post 9/11 America, and will share ideas for how to counter stereotypes and spread tolerance in their communities.

Note to Educators:
This lesson touches on a sensitive subject, and some words associated with negative stereotypes may come up in class during the suggested warm-up exercise. Students should be briefed on the difference between using such words in an academic versus a social setting, and should be advised to maintain a respectful environment throughout the lesson.

Procedure

1. Warm-up/Conversation Starters

Provide students with a definition of "stereotype."

As a class, brainstorm a list of groups based on religion, race, ethnicity, or social standing (e.g.: geeks, jocks, punks, etc.) on the board.

Next, divide students into four groups and have each group generate a list of slang words or visual stereotypes associated with a particular social group (they may draw from the list on the board).

Then, reconvene as a class and have students share their lists and reflect on the exercise. Some reflection questions you might ask include:

- Where did you hear or learn about these slang words and/or stereotypes? Are they positive, negative or neutral?

Grades
6-12

Subjects
- Current Events
- Fine Arts
- Journalism
- Language Arts
- Social Studies
- Media Studies

Materials Needed

a. *This Is Where I Need To be*—Chapters 6, 7, 8, and 10. Chapters 9 connect most strongly to this lesson. Other related chapters are 11, 13, 14, and 16.

b. Reproducible: "A Lesson from Santa" on page 59.

Key Terms
Islam, Muslim, Muslim American, prejudice, tolerance, essentialism, bias, stereotypes, stereotyping

Curriculum Guide & Reproducible Materials | 27

Stereotype (n.):
"A generalization about what people are like; an exaggerated image of their characteristics without regard to individual attributes"

- Do you know someone who is part of this group but doesn't fit this stereotype?

- Why do you think labels such as these exist in society?

- How do stereotypes and labels harm the people they are used to describe?

- What about the people who use them? How are they harmed by forming these stereotypes?

Tell students that they are going to examine the effects of stereotyping on one group of Americans—Muslim Americans.

2. Questions for Class Discussion

As a class, read and discuss the related chapters of *This is Where I Need to Be*, focusing on the following:

a. What is the critical event that these oral histories pinpoint as affecting the way the world views them? Find, highlight, or identify at least two quotes or examples to share with your classmates.

b. As you read these chapters, make a list of the common stereotypes associated with Muslims that the authors repeatedly encounter. In other words, what does the world seem to think a "real Muslim" is?

c. Is there a story in these oral histories that surprised you? That made you think differently about Muslim Americans than you did before? If yes, what is it? Explain how it affected you.

d. What solutions do these authors propose to counter the stereotypes that they bump up against in their schools and communities? Which of these actions do you think would be most successful and why?

e. Have you ever been in a situation similar to these authors where you have had to defend, justify, or explain your views, appearance, or behavior because another person assumed something about you? How did it feel?

3. Class Project

Divide students into small groups and provide each group with a copy of the reproducible **"A Lesson from Santa"** on page 59.

Ask students to look at the image closely and to discuss the following questions in their small groups:

- What do you think the artist's purpose was in creating this image?
- Who might her intended audience be?
- What impression does this image leave on you? Does it stir up a memory?

Reconvene as a class and invite students to share their impressions with each other. Share with them that this was a poster created by visual artist Cynthia Duxbury to address the negative power of stereotypes in post-9/11 America.

You may wish to share the following background information about the artist with students. It's excerpted from an article, "Unwrapping Stereotypes: Lessons from Santa" at **http://tinyurl.com/69xob9**:

> "I was looking at images of people in newspapers and books and started thinking how unfair it was, people just judging others on the way they look," she said. "I started to notice myself making some judgments on the people around me. I figured if I'm doing it, then a lot of other people are doing it, too."
>
> INS roundups, racial profiling, patriotism slipping into jingoism: Duxbury weighed it all as she created an image that played Santa's hat off the turban of a bearded, faceless man.
>
> "We have all been fed so much fear," Duxbury said.
>
> After creating the side-by-side Santa/turban images, Duxbury added the words: "Funny how the tiniest thing can make people feel different about you."

Related Resources

The following websites and organizations can provide additional background information and lesson ideas.

U.S. Religious Landscape Survey

Based on interviews with more than 35,000 American adults, this extensive survey by the Pew Forum on Religion & Public Life details the religious makeup, religious beliefs and practices as well as social and political attitudes of the American public, including the Muslim community.
http://religions.pewforum.org/

The Power of Words

A lesson plan from "Teaching Tolerance" that provides students with the opportunity to increase their awareness of the effects of using language that reinforces stereotypes.
http://tinyurl.com/6dsa2w

Hidden Bias: A Primer

A valuable resource from "Teaching Tolerance" with definitions of "stereotype" and "prejudice."
http://www.tolerance.org/hidden_bias/tutorials/index.html

Note:
An alternative lesson plan for this reproducible PDF is available at *http://tinyurl.com/5656hk*.

Duxbury emphasized that her message is less about politics and more about humanity. "It's common sense," she said. "I'm not very educated when it comes to political matters. This is about simple humanity."

Duxbury hopes people pause when they see her artwork, take a moment to think more deeply, moving beyond shallow, conditioned responses.

"It's about awareness and empathy," she said. "To stop and think, 'Gosh, maybe I looked at someone today and judged them when I shouldn't have.'"

After the group discussion, ask students to create their own posters to spread awareness about the harms of stereotyping. They can select any group from the list that was generated during the warm-up activity. Remind students that, like Duxbury, they should write a caption for their poster. You might also encourage them (especially if they're not comfortable drawing) to pull images and/or create a collage from a variety of media, including newspapers, magazines, and the Internet.

4. Homework & Assignments

a. Ask students to write an "artist's statement" to accompany their posters (some helpful guidelines are available at **http://tinyurl.com/3bs2wo**). You may wish to set up an exhibit in your classroom or in a prominent area of your school and invite students to present their work to their classmates or other members of the student body.

b. Select several images from the website (**http://www.ferris.edu/jimcrow/traveling2/THEM/**) of the traveling exhibition THEM: Images of Separation, which "showcases items from popular culture used to stereotype different groups, including Asian Americans, Hispanics, Jews and poor whites, as well as those who are 'other' in terms of body type or sexual orientation." (Note: some images include strong language so we definitely suggest that you vet the selections). Have students pick an image from your vetted list and ask them to describe the stereotype and research the historical period when such an image might have been created. This assignment should help students to view stereotyping and essentialism in a historical context.

c. Have students create a visual timeline of popular stereotypes in the United States. **Then ask them:**
   - In what ways can the types of stereotyping and ethnic, racial, or religious profiling and harassment be remedied?
   - What can we do as individuals and as communities?

   Divide the class into groups and invite students to come up with action plans for an anti-bias project with clear start and end dates, goals, and benchmarks. This project could extend over the course of a quarter or semester so that students might see the impact of their vision. Possible projects might include: creating a school club to learn about world cultures and religions; organizing Diwali or Eid celebrations and inviting guest speakers; volunteering with a refugee program and getting to know Muslim arrivals; forming a book club to read books about the Muslim or minority experience in America.

d. The Pew Forum on Religion & Public Life published its "U.S. Religious Landscape Survey" in 2008. The document "Beliefs Portrait of Muslims" offers a summary of the diversity of Muslims beliefs. It is available at **http://religions.pewforum.org/pdf/beliefs_portrait-Muslims.pdf.** Have students evaluate the findings of this study and write an essay about why it counters stereotypes.

e. The website *Change the Story* (www.changethestory.net) is an online resource aimed at transforming harmful stereotypes about Muslims that persist in society. It offers an interactive experience where users—Muslim and non-Muslim alike—can meet their neighbors, learn about Islam and apply techniques of interfaith dialogue and action to local communities. Have students browse this website and its videos "Meet Your Neighbor." Then, ask them to research a prominent American Muslim or go out into their community and interview a Muslim community member. They can write up their research or make a short video modeled on "Meet Your Neighbor."

Related Resources

Who Are the Arab Americans?
This activity is designed to increase student knowledge about Arab Americans and to challenge misperceptions students might hold about Arabs and people of Arab descent.
http://tinyurl.com/5vyoka

Young Video Makers Try to Alter Islam's Face
May 8, 2008 New York Times article about a new wave of young American Muslim performers and filmmakers trying to change the public face of their religion.
http://www.nytimes.com/2008/05/08/us/08video.html

One Nation, Many Voices
Award winners of the annual film contest, sponsored by Link TV, which invites American Muslims to make short films about "stories, not stereotypes."
http://www.linktv.org/onenation
http://www.linktv.org/onenation2007/winners

I am a Muslim
Murad Amayreh's "I Am a Muslim" video tries to contradict stereotypes with a man named Muhammad who presents himself as an ordinary American. It has attracted over two million hits on YouTube.
http://tinyurl.com/2x2ulu

Related Resources

Facing History

A wealth of resources and articles are available at the website of this non-profit organization whose aim is to "engage students of diverse backgrounds in an examination of racism, prejudice, and anti-semitism in order to promote the development of a more humane and informed citizenry."
http://www.facinghistory.org/resources/facingtoday/33

Teachers Against Prejudice

A non-profit group which helps teachers address issues of sensitivity and respect concerning diversity in the classroom and provides trained professionals to teach students how to confront prejudice.
http://www.teachersagainstprejudice.org/

5. Assessment

Teacher evaluation of classroom participation. Teachers may wish to develop additional rubrics and measures for class projects and longer-term assignments.

6. National Standards

These academic standards are drawn from the *Mid-Continent Research for Education and Learning's "Content Knowledge: A Compendium of Standards and Benchmarks for K-12 Education: 3rd and 4th Editions."*

Grades 6-12

- *Behavioral Studies Standard 1:* Understands that group and cultural influences contribute to human development, identity, and behavior.
- *Behavioral Studies Standard 2:* Understands various meanings of social group, general implications of group membership, and different ways that groups function.
- *Civics Standard 11:* Understands the role of diversity in American life and the importance of shared values, political beliefs, and civic beliefs in an increasingly diverse American society.
- *Language Arts Standard 1:* Demonstrates competence in the general skills and strategies of the writing process.
- *Language Arts Standard 7:* Demonstrates competence in the general skills and strategies for reading a variety of informational texts.
- *Language Arts Standard 8:* Demonstrates competence in speaking and listening as tools for learning.
- *United States History Standard 31:* Understands economic, social, and cultural developments in the contemporary United States.

Lesson Plan: **The ID Project**

Exploring Identity Through the Lens of Culture and Religion

Overview

In this lesson, students will define "identity" and consider how it (a) can be shaped by religion and culture and (b) can shape morals, values, and social interactions.

Procedure

1. Warm-up/Conversation Starters

Write the word "identity" on the board and ask students to brainstorm its meanings. Keep track of students' responses with a concept or **mind map** (see sidebar). Students will most likely begin to call out answers that fall into the following categories, among others:

- possessions or material objects
- interests
- people/family
- community
- character traits
- personality
- goals
- ethnicity
- religion
- geography

Grades
6-12

Subjects
- Civics
- American History
- Language Arts
- Media Studies
- Social Studies
- Global History

Materials Needed

a. *This Is Where I Need To be*—Chapters 5, 14, 16, 18, and 20 connect most strongly to this theme. Other related chapters are 1, 2, 3, 5, 7, 8, 10, 11, 15, 16, 18, 19, 21, 22, and 23.

b. Reproducible: "Identity Chart" on page 61.

Key Terms

identity, Islam, multi-cultural, diversity, teens, Muslims in America, African American Muslims, ethnocentrism

Curriculum Guide & Reproducible Materials | 33

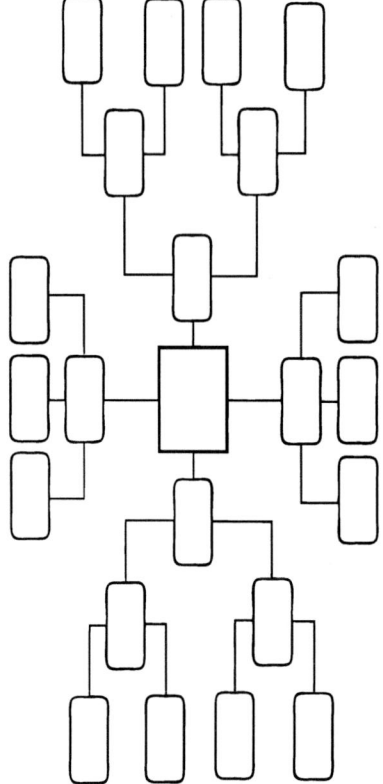

A concept or mind map is an organizing and brainstorming device where single words are enclosed in a rectangle and are connected to other concept boxes by arrows. Major concept boxes will have lines to and from several other concept boxes generating a network.

This example was taken from **mymindmap.com,** a site featuring a number of mind map templates.

A question you might ask is whether identity is just another word for asking, "Who am I on the inside? Who am I on the outside?" Using this question as a springboard, have students explore what identity means for someone like President Barack Obama (of course, there are many prominent and well-known figures you might use for this activity).

Ask students to call out attributes of President Obama's identity by thinking about the question: What makes Barack Obama who he is on the inside and the outside? Make a list on the board. Some answers that might come up may include: bi-racial, Hawaii, Kenya, Indonesia, his love of basketball, his hometown of Chicago, politician, lawyer, father, husband, Harvard graduate and now President. Through your questions, you're making clear to students that all these are parts of Obama's identity.

Wrap-up the activity by sharing the following definition of identity with students:

> Identity is our sense of who we are. It is formed by a combination of many factors, including social ties such as our connections to a family, an ethnic group, a religion, a community, a school, or a nation. Our personal experiences also affect our identity. So do our values and beliefs.

Share with students that they are going to be reading and discussing oral histories where identity plays an important part in people's views of and interactions with the world.

2. Questions for Class Discussion

As a class, read and discuss the related chapters in *This is Where I Need to Be*, focusing on the following:

a. Pick two oral histories from the book and compare the factors or characteristics the writers most associate with their identities. What do they have in common? How are they different? (Note to teachers: You may wish to use a Venn diagram for this question.)

b. How do religion, culture, and world events shape the identities of the authors featured in the book? Why do you think this is so? What about you? How do these factors impact or shape your identity?

c. What do these stories tell you about the impact of the world on people's identities? Does society or community change the way people perceive themselves? Find a passage from one of the oral histories to support your answer.

d. On **page 73**, Nurah Ahmad recounts her experiences at both a public school and a Muslim private school. How do you think her time spent at both institutions strengthen her identity?

e. Do these stories lead you to conclude that identity is static or ever-evolving? Multifaceted or one-sided? Explain your answer by using examples from the oral histories for support.

f. Did you see aspects of yourself reflected in these stories? Do you better understand someone or yourself after reading these stories? Why or why not?

3. Class Project

Have students use the "Identity Chart" reproducible on page 61 to map out their own identities. Once they have finished, they should answer the following questions either in their journals or in a group discussion:

a. Underline or highlight the most important aspects of your identity.

b. How have words or phrases that others use to describe you shaped your identity?

c. What aspects of your identity are most relevant when it comes to making important decisions such as how you dress, what movies or TV shows you watch, or who your friends are?

Have students repeat this activity by mapping out the identity of one of the authors from *This is Where I Need to Be*. They should answer the above questions in context of the writer's oral history, using the identity chart and oral history as source material.

Wrap up this activity by having students discuss how dissecting identity made them view themselves, their classmates, and the authors of *This is Where I Need to Be* differently.

Related Resources

The following materials offer more information on identity and the Muslim American experience.

"The Koran, punk rock and lots of questions," by Erika Hayasaki

A compelling feature article and photo essay (November 19, 2008) from The Los Angeles Times about Muslim American teenagers search for identity.
http://tinyurl.com/6b5wab

Islamic Learning

This photo essay from Time magazine takes us inside an Illinois school where "two worlds" meet.
http://www.time.com/time/photoessays/muslimschool/

Muslim in America

An intimate portrait of America's Muslim community, also from Time magazine.
http://tinyurl.com/6ymoas

To Be Muslim

Boston Globe photographer Christopher Churchill's photo essay of Muslims from across the Boston area, with text and audio about their conversations ranging from women and independence to peace and violence to the role of religion in their lives.
http://tinyurl.com/5shwva

Related Resources

Muslim American: A New Identity? By Ruhi Hamid
An article from BBC News about what it means to be Muslim and American in a post 9/11 world.
http://tinyurl.com/6s6pag

Muslim Girl
This magazine explores identity, culture, fashion, and religion for Muslim girls in the West.
http://www.muslimgirlworld.com/

Islam Overview
A brief overview on Islam from CNN.
http://tinyurl.com/6a2fl5

Islam
MSN Encarta article on Islam
http://encarta.msn.com/encyclopedia_761579171/islam.html

Reporting on Religion: A Primer for Journalists
Religion Newswriters provides a thorough introduction to Islam for religion journalists. This may also be helpful in the classroom.
http://www.rnasecure.org/guide/islam.html

4. Homework & Assignments

a. Ask students to use the words they generated in their "Identity Chart" to write an "I Am From" poem both for themselves as well as for an author from This Is Where I Need To Be (preferably, the author's whose identity they have already mapped out using the "Identity Chart"). See a sample "I Am From" poem by poet George Ella Lyon and instructions for how to write it at **www.georgeellalyon.com/where.html**.

b. Have students create a website or exhibit titled "Islam 101." Their exhibit should include the following:

1. What are the Five Pillars of Islam?
2. Who is the main figure in Islam?
3. What is the main language in Islam?
4. Some moral teachings, quotes, or sayings from Islam.
5. Who are Muslims? A pie chart showing the countries of origin of American Muslims.
6. Photographs of Muslims in America that show dual identities.
7. Images of American mosques.

Engage students in a class discussion about how these factors shape the identity of an American Muslim.

c. Have students read and discuss the following personal essays by Muslim Americans from the NPR series, "This I Believe":
1. **"We Are Each Other's Business" by Eboo Patel**
   http://www.npr.org/templates/story/story.php?storyId=4989625
2. **"The Right to be Fully American" by Yasir Billoo**
   http://www.npr.org/templates/story/story.php?storyId=6608111

Ask students to write their own "This I Believe" essays about their identities.

d. Ask students to list any seven nations that have Muslim majorities, beginning with the nation with the largest Muslim population. They should research the languages spoken there and list their neighboring nations. Then, students should investigate how religious identity can be impacted by one's culture, citing examples from the oral histories in *This is Where I Need to Be* as evidence.

e. Have students read **"The Koran, punk rock and lots of questions"** by Erika Hayasaki. This article in the November 19, 2008 issue of The Los Angeles Times takes an in-depth look at Muslim American youth's search for identity. It is available online at http://tinyurl.com/6b5wab. After students have read the article, ask them to write an essay comparing it to the oral histories in *This Is Where I Need To Be*. What are the common themes and issues faced by the youths featured in both works?

f. Explain to students that they will be investigating the idea of identity and what it means in the context of African American Muslims. Provide them with the following articles from Common Ground News and divide them into small groups to discuss how identity and faith co-mingle in the African American Muslim community.

1. **"A Royal Heritage" by Sheik Anwar Muhaimin**
   An article about how an African Muslim used his faith and African heritage to keep from indulging in the "blame game" and instead taking responsibility for his own actions and related outcomes.
   http://tinyurl.com/689lrk

2. **"African Americans Help Diminish Islamophobia" by Faheem Shuaibe**
   Having faced derisive stereotyping before, the author elaborates on why he feels African American Muslims can stem the tide of Islamophobia.
   http://tinyurl.com/6la47b

3. **"African American Muslims refute the clash of civilizations" by Dawud Walid**
   This article chronicles the ways in which the Civil Rights Movement and African American Muslims paved the way for Muslim immigrants to America.
   http://tinyurl.com/6syk5v

Related Resources

U.S. Religious Landscape Survey
Based on interviews with more than 35,000 American adults, this extensive survey by the Pew Forum on Religion & Public Life details the religious makeup, religious beliefs and practices as well as social and political attitudes of the American public, including the Muslim community. *http://religions.pewforum.org/*

Does My Head Look Big in This, by Randa Abdel-Fattah
In this novel (Scholastic, 2008), 16-year-old Amal makes the decision to start wearing the hijab and must deal with the all the reactions—from her parents, her teachers, her friends, people on the street.

Muslims in Metropolis, by Kavitha Rajagopalan
A thorough and insightful examination (Rutgers University Press, 2008) of the identity formation and experiences of three very different Muslim families in the West – in London, New York, and Berlin. This is a good read for college and adult audiences, but excerpts would work in the classroom as well because of the author's journalistic style.

After they have read these articles, ask students to write a paper on ways in which the Civil Rights Movement and African American Muslims have paved the way for Muslim immigrants to America. When students have completed their assignment, reconvene as a large group to review their conclusions. To wrap up the activity, ask students to highlight the dual identities that Muslims in *This is Where I Need to Be* have and how they perceive themselves.

5. Assessment

Teacher evaluation of classroom participation. Teachers may wish to develop additional rubrics and measures for class projects and longer-term assignments.

6. National Standards

- *Behavioral Studies Standard 1:* Understands that group and cultural influences contribute to human development, identity, and behavior.
- *Behavioral Studies Standard 2:* Understands various meanings of social group, general implications of group membership, and different ways that groups function.
- *Language Arts Standard 1:* Demonstrates competence in the general skills and strategies of the writing process.
- *Language Arts Standard 7:* Demonstrates competence in the general skills and strategies for reading a variety of informational texts.
- *Language Arts Standard 8:* Demonstrates competence in speaking and listening as tools for learning.
- *United States History Standard 31:* Understands economic, social, and cultural developments in the contemporary United States.

Lesson Plan: **Choices, Choices**

Considering the Pros and Cons of Peer Pressure

Overview

In this lesson, students will consider the impact of peer pressure on adolescent life, and will then debate its pros and cons.

Procedure

1. Warm-up/Conversation Starters

Place a large number of beans in a glass jar. Ask students to guess the number of beans in the jar and to anonymously write down their answers on a scrap of paper. Collect their responses. Then, divide the class into three groups and ask each group to guess the number of beans in the jar. Provide each group with a sheet of paper to write their response:

- **For Group 1:** Provide some high estimates for them to consider
- **For Group 2:** Provide some low estimates for them to consider
- **For Group 3:** Provide no estimates for them to consider

Collect each group's response, and then tell them the correct answer. Ask students to consider how their guesses were affected by the estimates they were provided (or not). The results of this experiment should show that students were more likely to guess numbers in a certain range depending upon the estimate provided to their group.

Share with students the range of guesses that they individually came up with at the start of the activity (it should be quite wide). Ask the class: Did the group discussion sway your opinion one way or another? Why do you think so many of you came up with such a range of different answers when I originally asked you to just look at the jar and write down a number by yourselves?

Grades
6-12

Subjects
- Civics
- Fine Arts
- Language Arts
- Sociology

Materials Needed

a. *This Is Where I Need To be*— Chapters 3, 10, 12, and 18 connect most strongly to this lesson, as does Quainat Zaman's personal reflection. Other related chapters are 14 and 22.

b. Jar of beans (jelly beans, coffee beans, lentils, etc.).

Key Terms

identity, temptations, Muslim youth, Five Pillars, conflict resolution, group behavior, peer pressure

Peer Pressure (n.):
Social pressure from members of a group to accept certain beliefs or act in certain ways in order to be accepted

Share with students that a similar experiment was originally conducted back in 1932 by psychologist Arthur Jenness who found that when the number of beans was estimated by people on their own there was quite a wide range of numbers given. However, when groups were given an estimate, the range of numbers grew narrower.

Ask: Why do you think that is?

Share a definition of **peer pressure** with students. Then ask: In what other areas of your life do you feel influenced by your peers' opinions or actions in both helpful and harmful ways? Make a list of responses on the board in two columns: "pros" and "cons."

Wrap-up the activity by telling students that they are going to be reading and discussing oral histories that explore the impact of peer pressure on the experiences and self-esteem of young Muslim Americans.

2. Questions for Class Discussion

As a class, read and discuss the related chapters in *This is Where I Need to Be,* focusing on the following:

a. What types of peer pressure and temptations do the writers of *This is Where I Need to Be* face? Make a list.

b. Identify or highlight a passage that captures the conflict faced by one of the authors.

c. How do these authors deal with the peer pressure in their lives? To what do they turn for strength or support?

d. Did you come across any examples where peer pressure was a positive force in the lives of these authors? If yes, what and how?

e. Were you able to identify with the experiences shared by these oral histories? Why or why not?

3. Class Project

Ask students to research the Five Pillars of Islamic faith as well as some of Islam's cultural norms (e.g.: no dating, no alcohol). Keeping these in mind, prompt students to write "Dear Abby" style letters about possible peer pressure dilemmas that young Muslim Americans might encounter. They might also wish to write from the point of view of one of the authors in *This is Where I Need to Be*.

Put all of the letters into a hat and have each student pick one letter. Tell students that they will play the role of an advice columnist and will write a response to the letter they've chosen, offering counsel and tips on how to deal with the given situation in school or their community. They might also focus on how to turn a difficult situation into a positive one. Invite students to find examples of positive, hip, and cool role models to cite as proof that it is possible to follow one's path of individuality.

Wrap up by having students reflect on how this activity allowed them to "walk in another's shoes," so to speak, or helped them come up with solutions to peer pressure that make sense in their own lives. You may also want to open up the discussion to the question of how their faith impacts their own choices.

4. Homework & Assignments

a. Have students read Robert Frost's poem "The Road Not Taken" and pick an oral history from *This is Where I Need to Be*. Ask students to write a journal entry from the perspective of the oral history's author about a situation in his or her life where a lifestyle or decision went against the grain. What might this person have experienced? What gave him or her strength during this time? Was it worthwhile or not? Students may find it helpful to conduct some research to better understand the author's particular situation.

b. Ask students to write and perform a play on the theme of peer pressure where the main character struggles with a moral or ethical dilemma. They may choose to use one of the oral histories in *This Is Where I Need To Be* as inspiration for their play.

Related Resources

The following websites and organizations can provide additional background information and lesson ideas.

Peer Pressure

An article in The Guardian about Solomon Asch's famous peer pressure experiment in the 1950s.
http://tinyurl.com/6dt4ta

eMints

Classroom resources on peer pressure from eMints National Center.
http://www.emints.org/ethemes/resources/S00000458.shtml

"Peer Pressure Marketing," by Thessaly La Force

Article about Youth Radio poll which found that peer pressure is the most effective form of marketing.
http://tinyurl.com/5famta

Related Resources

"The ABCs of Conflict Resolution"

This useful lesson plan from "Teaching Tolerance" looks at the way in-group favoritism hurts instead of heals conflicts. *http://tinyurl.com/5oxu7p*

Does My Head Look Big in This, by Randa Abdel-Fattah

In this novel (Scholastic, 2008), 16-year-old Amal makes the decision to start wearing the hijab and must deal with peer pressure from strangers and her community.

---

c. Ask students to select and read a novel that explores themes of peer pressure and individuality. A good list of young adult novels is available at http://www.librarything.com/tag/peer+pressure. Then have students write book reviews and post the reviews in the school library or publish them on a blog.

d. Invite students to write essays about a time in their lives when they took "the road less traveled." Host a "memoir café" in your classroom where students share their essays.

e. Have students write modern fables (modeled after Aesop) in which the main character learns a lesson about dealing with peer pressure. Compile and publish these in a class publication.

5. Assessment

Teacher evaluation of classroom participation. Teachers may wish to develop additional rubrics and measures for class projects and longer-term assignments.

6. National Standards

These academic standards are drawn from the *Mid-Continent Research for Education and Learning's "Content Knowledge: A Compendium of Standards and Benchmarks for K-12 Education: 3rd and 4th Editions."*

Grades 6-12

- *Behavioral Studies Standard 1:* Understands that group and cultural influences contribute to human development, identity, and behavior.
- *Behavioral Studies Standard 2:* Understands various meanings of social group, general implications of group membership, and different ways that groups function.
- *Language Arts Standard 1:* Demonstrates competence in the general skills and strategies of the writing process.
- *Language Arts Standard 7:* Demonstrates competence in the general skills and strategies for reading a variety of informational texts.
- *Language Arts Standard 8:* Demonstrates competence in speaking and listening as tools for learning.

Related Resources

I Believe In...Christian, Jewish, and Muslim Young People Speak About Their Faith, by Pearl Fuyo Gaskins

This collection (Cricket Books, 2004) features interviews with and profiles of 15- to 24-year-olds on the personal meaning of their faiths.

Dear Author: Letters of Hope, edited by Joan Kaywell

In this 2007 compilation of letters (Philomel, 2007), teen writers write to and receive replies from top young adult authors about the toughest issues they face, including peer pressure, bullying, and ostracism.

Reproducibles

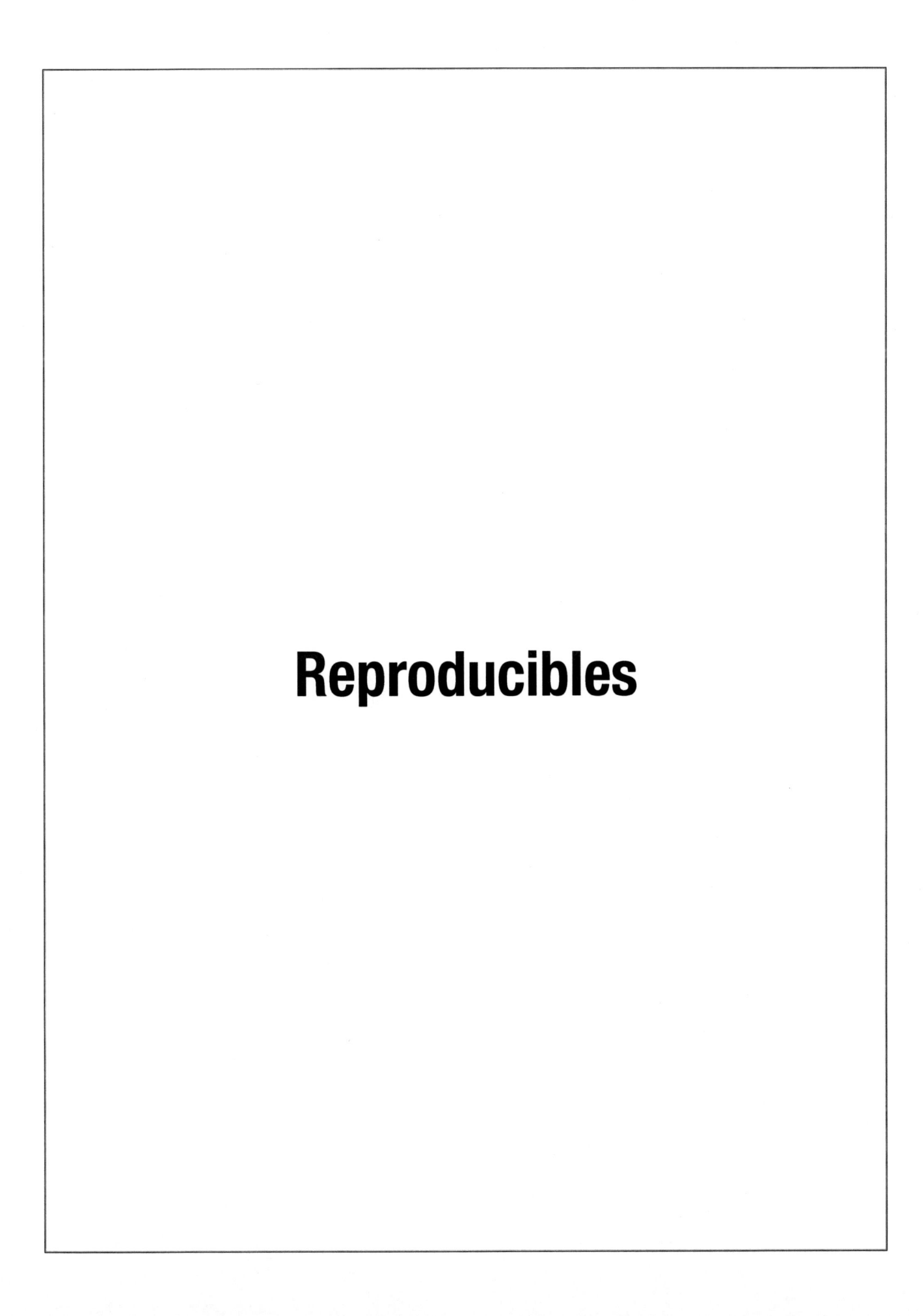

Name _____ Date _____

Tabs on the Media

Directions: *Use the following chart to record and analyze coverage of a particular ethnic or religious group in news or online media (you may use the back of this page if you need more room). On a separate sheet of paper, paste images or quotes that stand out to you.*

Date of Coverage	Source	Headline/ Summary	Key words or images	Is this a positive or negative depiction of the group? Explain.

So What?

What connotations (implied meanings) do these words and images have? Are they positive, negative, or neutral? How do they harm the people in that (minority) group? How do they harm the people outside of that group? How has this exercise made you think differently about the ways in which you perceive of a group of people?

Curriculum Guide & Reproducible Materials | 47

Wall of Fame: **Personalities**

Directions for educators: Below is a list of notable historical, literary, political, and cultural figures, all of whom happen to be Muslim. Cut out names and ask students to draw one each at random

Shirin Ebadi (Nobel Prize winner)	**Mohammad Alexander Russell Webb** (Muslim from Victorian America)	**Aron Kader** (comic)	**Yusuf Islam** (singer-songwriter)
Farah Ahmedi (author)	**Muhammad Ali** (world boxing champ)	**Maz Jobrani** (comic)	**Native Deen** (RAP group)
Diana Abu-Jaber (author)	**Malcolm X** (Civil Rights leader)	**Ahmed Ahmed** (comic)	**Seven8Six** (pop band)
Mo Amer (comic)	**Ibn Battuta** (historical figure)	**Abdul-Karim al-Jabbar** (former NFL player)	**Averroes** (historical figure)
Preacher Moss (comic)	**Keith Ellison** (U.S. politician)	**Haroon Siddiqui** (editor, author)	**Dawud Wharnsby** (singer-songwriter)
Azhar Usman (comic)	**Dr. Eboo Patel** (visionary)	**Ryan Harris** (football player)	**Zarqa Nawaz** (filmmaker)
Rukhsana Khan (author)	**Shazia Mirza** (comic)	**Andre Carson** (Congressman)	**Roqaya Al-Gassra** (athlete)
Naguib Mahfouz (author, Nobel Prize winner)	**Mohammad Yunus** (Nobel Prize winner)	**Hakeem Abdul Olajuwon** (retired NBA player)	**Ali Velshi** (CNN journalist)
Kareem Abdul-Jabbar (former NBA Player)	**Salman Rushdie** (author)	**Ibn Khaldun** (historical figure)	**Orhan Pamuk** (novelist, Nobel Prize winner)

Copyright Student Press Initiative 2008 • www.thisiswhereineedtobe.com

Curriculum Guide & Reproducible Materials | 49

Name _____ Date _____

Wall of Fame: **Research Notes**

Directions: *Use this handout to help you conduct your research on a prominent historical, political or social figure and member of the Muslim community. Use additional pages if needed. When you complete your research, use a separate sheet of paper to write a 200-300 word biography of this individual for your classroom's Muslim Wall of Fame.*

1. What is the name of the individual you are researching?

....

2. Use this space to take notes on important biographical details about this person, e.g.: date of birth, age, hometown, profession, education, etc.

....

....

....

3. List his or her major accomplishments.

....

....

....

4. List a few quotes from the person you are researching or write down some things that people have to say about him or her.

....

....

....

5. What did you learn about this person and/or their work that inspired you?

....

....

....

Copyright Student Press Initiative 2008 • www.thisiswhereineedtobe.com

Name _____ Date _____

Wall of Fame: **Profile**

Directions: Use this handout to create a Wall of Fame profile after completing your research.

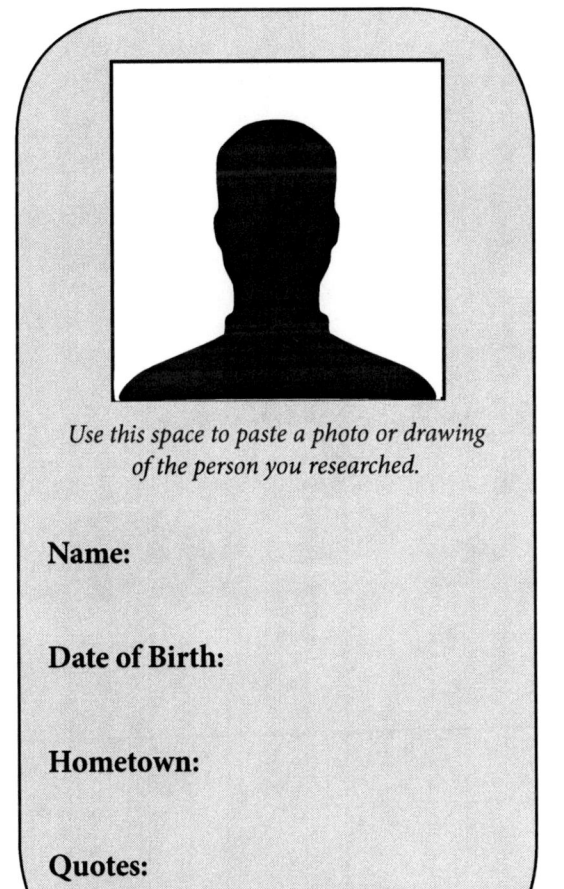

Use this space to paste a photo or drawing of the person you researched.

Name:

Date of Birth:

Hometown:

Quotes:

Interests _____
_____
_____

Best Known For _____
_____
_____
_____

Major Accomplishments _____
_____
_____
_____

Most Inspiring Quality _____
_____
_____

Use this space to create a collage or paste images of objects that reflect this person's personality, career, interests or accomplishments.

Use this space to paste the lyrics to a song that you think this person would listen to and/or that you think reflects his or her life or accomplishments.

Copyright Student Press Initiative 2008 • www.thisiswhereineedtobe.com

Curriculum Guide & Reproducible Materials | 53

A Lesson from Santa

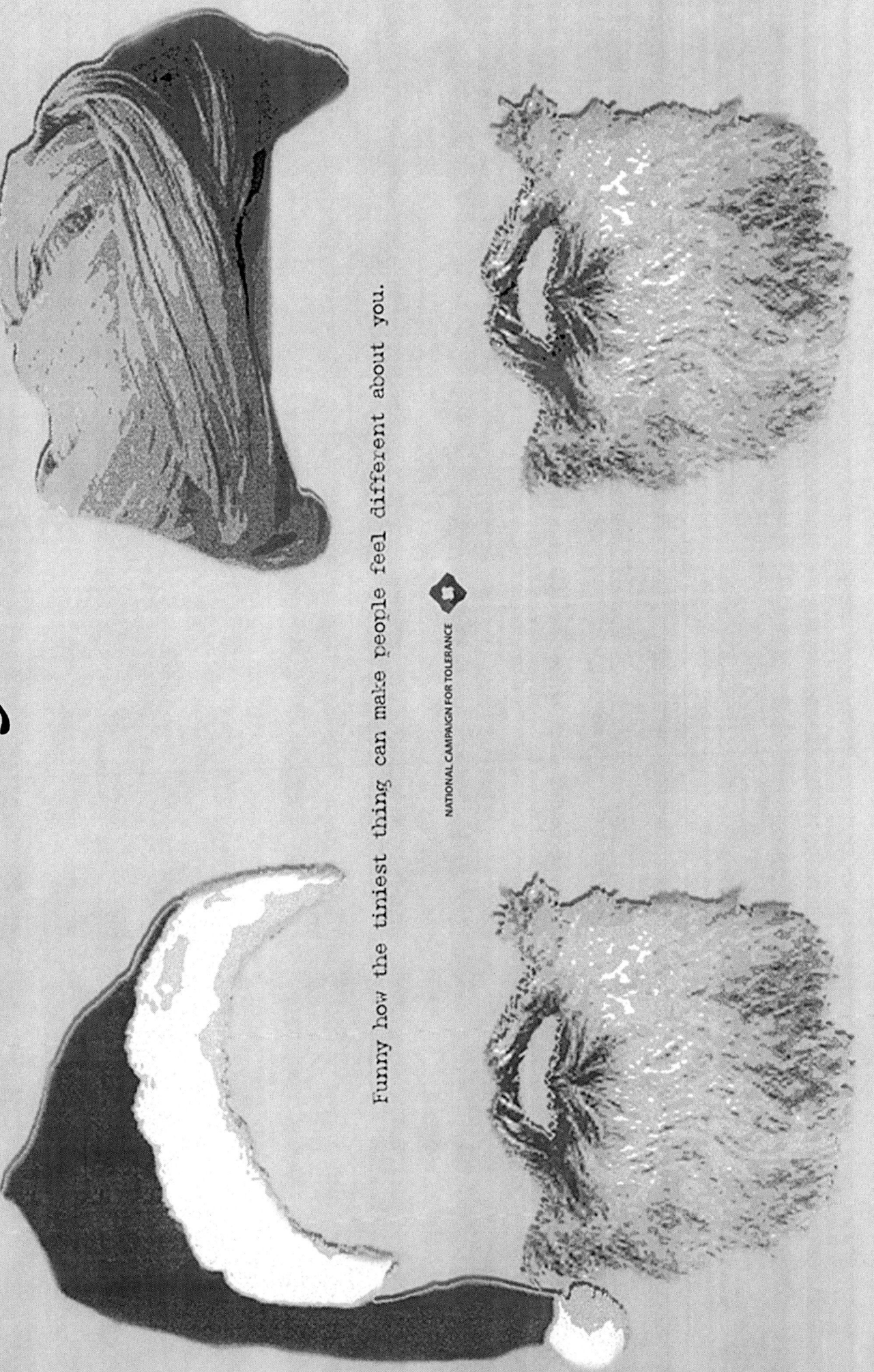

Funny how the tiniest thing can make people feel different about you.

NATIONAL CAMPAIGN FOR TOLERANCE

www.tolerance.org

Name _____ Date _____

Identity Chart

Directions: *Fill in the following spaces with words or phrases that best describe your identity or the identity of the person you're interviewing.*

LIFE CIRCUMSTANCES:
Major events that have shaped who I am today.

PHILOSOPHY:
Values and beliefs about the world that shape me.

OTHERS:
Words and phrases that others use to desribe me.

ME:
Words and phrases that you use to desribe yourself.

WHO ARE YOU?

Paste a picture of yourself here

Copyright Student Press Initiative 2008 • www.thisiswhereineedtobe.com

Curriculum Guide & Reproducible Materials | 57

Say It Out Loud: **An Oral History Primer for Educators**

What is Oral History?

Oral history is an interactive and living method of research that relies upon the memories of "real life" individuals and firsthand accounts of past and/or current events. It is a personal word-for-word account of one's own story—often focusing on a specific time period or event— and is a powerful method by which eyewitnesses or their descendents remember the day-to-day experiences of people, families and societies.

One of the oldest oral history projects in American schools is the Foxfire Project begun in 1966 by Eliot Wigginton, a teacher in the Appalachian Mountains. His students interviewed elders in their rural community and used the information they gathered to paint a picture of an important period in history as told through the stories and memories of people who lived during that time.

The resulting oral history project was printed in magazine form and later developed into a series of books, the first of which was titled *The Foxfire Book: Hog Dressing, Log Cabin Building, Mountain Crafts and Foods, Planting by the Signs, Snake Lore, Hunting Tales, Faith Healing, Moonshining* (Anchor Books, 1972). Since then, the Foxfire Project has taken on many forms and shapes in schools across the United States.

Today, the Student Press Initiative (SPI) at Teachers College, Columbia University is a leading publisher of student oral histories including: *This is Where I Need to Be: Oral Histories of Muslim Youth in New York City; Linking Literature: Using Oral History to Connect Books to the World; Speak to Us of Work: Bronx Oral Histories;* and the *Killing the Sky: Oral Histories from Horizon Academy, Rikers Island* series. In partnership with local schools, SPI helps to develop curricula and build publication-rich school communities where every student is encouraged to publish out of one or more disciplines. In SPI's model of teaching writing for publication, students learn imperative skills in drafting, revising and copyediting through real-life models of working.

If you are interested in learning more about SPI and the program's publications, please visit their website at www.publishspi.org.

Why Oral History?

While much of written history is based on tangible evidence such as printed texts, documents and sound recordings, some histories can only be known through oral narratives. Oral history is an opportunity to involve the everyday person in the writing of history.

Oral history is a research method that empowers young adults. Oral history methodology and techniques are easily adaptable to middle school and high school classrooms. Students can use it to archive important events in their own families, neighborhoods or local communities. The student oral historian is empowered by the act of documenting and preserving the memories and perspectives of ordinary people whose voices might otherwise be forgotten.

While oral histories have been traditionally collected for archival purposes in which unedited transcripts of interviews are preserved as historical records, many teachers today incorporate a new style of oral history writing into their classrooms. This new take on the genre, which one might call "crafted oral history," can be traced back to the work of Studs Terkel, a well-known radio personality and oral historian who made a career out of interviewing people around the United States about their experiences with topics such as race, faith, work, the Great Depression and World War II. In crafted oral history, a student works with the transcript and makes decisions about what to leave in and take out as well as how to organize the text. The act of "revising" the oral history, then, asks students to balance the interview subject's language and voice with the "readability," grammar and conventions of a written text.

In your classroom, an oral history project can engage students in various stages of the research and writing process in the following ways:

- *Research:* Students research a topic for their oral history project and become familiar with a period or event in history, a current social situation, or a community.

- *Interviewing:* Students choose an individual or individuals to interview and learn both how to craft effective questions as well as the skills needed to conduct an interview.

- *Transcribing:* Students listen to their recorded interviews and learn to accurately transcribe those sections that best relate to their themes or research topics. They also study how to capture spoken language in writing.

- *Writing and Editing:* Students create a rough draft of their oral history. They learn how to take out interviewer's questions from transcripts and make sure that the subject's words still make sense. They arrange the oral history and develop a structure that flows logically and smoothly.

They learn to remove filler words and add parenthetical asides to give the reader further information about the subject, the theme, or the interview itself.

- *Revising*: Students share and review their oral histories with their peers and teacher—and often the oral history subject as well— for clarity, structure, accuracy and impact. They make changes and revisions based on the feedback they receive.

- *Publishing*: Students create a finished product based on the results of their oral history survey.

For more, see *Project Notes: Conducting Oral History in the Secondary Classroom* (Student Press Initiative, 2005) by Kerry McKibbin.

Interviewing Skills

A good interview makes the subject feel comfortable and invites him or her to tap into memories and share rich details of his or her life. Following are some tips that will help your students generate a list of successful interview questions:

- Make a list of topics you want to know about.
- Prepare questions that will address these topics.
- Phrase your questions so that they are open-ended and don't elicit a "yes" or "no" answer.
- Prompt your subject with questions that use phrases such as "tell me about…, " "explain to me…," "talk to me about your feelings on…."
- Avoid complicated and long questions. Keep it simple.
- Stay neutral. Don't ask "leading" questions that make your subject feel as if there's a right or wrong answer.
- Group your questions together in an order that seems logical.
- Don't be afraid to switch things around or interrupt your question order during the interview.
- Sometimes you won't be able to anticipate the direction in which a conversation will go and following-up with a question will prove to be key to unearthing your subject's story.
- Don't interrupt responses.
- Ask for visual descriptions of people, places, or objects.
- Don't be afraid of silence. Sometimes your subject will want to pause and reflect.

More interview suggestions and a question generator are available at the StoryCorps website at http://www.storycorps.net/record-your-story/question-generator/list.

Resources

Oral History Collections

Remembering Slavery: African Americans Talk About Their Personal Experiences of Slavery and Emancipation, by Ira Berlin, Marc Favreau, and Steven Miller

This book and audio set (The New Press, 1999) features transcripts of 124 former slaves interviewed in the 1920s and 1930s along with recently restored recorded interviews from the Library of Congress.
http://www.amazon.com/Remembering-Slavery-Americans-Experiences-Emancipation/dp/1595582282

Strange Ground: Americans in Vietnam, 1945-1975, by Harry Maurer

This oral history (Henry Holt, 1989) traces the evolution of American involvement from the last days of World War II to the fall of Saigon three decades later.
http://www.amazon.com/Strange-Ground-Americans-Vietnam-History/dp/B000TCXJ7U

Twilight: Los Angeles, 1992, by Anna Deavere Smith

A compelling play (Anchor Books, 1993) that uses verbatim the words of people who experienced the Los Angeles riots of 1992.
http://www.amazon.com/Twilight-Angeles-Anna-Deavere-Smith/dp/0822218410

Hard Times: An Oral History of the Great Depression, by Studs Terkel

First published in 1970, this classic of oral history (The New Press, 2000) by Pulitzer Prize-winning writer and journalist Studs Terkel features the voices of men and women who lived through the Great Depression of the 1930s.
http://www.amazon.com/Hard-Times-History-Great-Depression/dp/1565846567

Working: People Talk About What They Do All Day and How They Feel About What They Do, by Studs Terkel

A classic collection (The New Press, 1997) of oral history reflections on the working life from men and women from all walks of life.
http://www.amazon.com/Working-People-Talk-About-What/dp/1565843428

Killing the Sky Volumes 1, 2, 3, and 4

From Student Press Initiative comes a powerful collection (2005) of oral histories featuring inmates at Horizon Academy on Rikers Island.

Vol 1: http://www.lulu.com/content/1594914
Vol 2: http://www.lulu.com/content/1338875
Vol 3: http://www.lulu.com/content/1269577
Vol 4: http://www.lulu.com/content/2334259

Linking Literature: Using Oral History to Connect Books to the World, by Eighth Grade Students at the NYC Lab School for Collaborative Studies

A book of student-written oral histories (Student Press Initiative, 2004) that explore thematic connections between historical literary texts and our contemporary society, using Harper Lee's *To Kill a Mockingbird* as an entry point. Subjects range from the unknown to the famous, and include Holocaust survivors, local political figures and renowned journalist Bill Moyers.
http://www.lulu.com/content/1371954

The Foxfire Book: Hog Dressing, Log Cabin Building, Mountain Crafts and Foods, Planting by the Signs, Snake Lore, Hunting Tales, Faith Healing, Moonshining, edited by Eliot Wigginton

This first compilation of oral histories (Anchor Books, 1972) collected by students records and preserves the traditional folk culture of the Southern Appalachians. It is one in a series of subsequent volumes.
http://www.amazon.com/Foxfire-Book-Dressing-Building-Moonshining/dp/0385073534

Crossing the BLVD: Strangers, Neighbors, Aliens in a New America by Judith Sloan and Warren Lehrer

A collection of first-person narratives (W. W. Norton & Co, 2004) from inhabitants of the country's most diverse borough, Queens. First-person narratives that sometimes intertwine several voices (some were broadcast on the public radio program *The Next Big Thing*) are matched by a bold and colorful layout: large portraits, long-view landscapes, multiple typefaces (sometimes within the same paragraph) and inset graphics or asides This book comes with an audio CD that includes interview excerpts.
http://www.amazon.com/Crossing-BLVD-Strangers-Neighbors-America/dp/0393324664

Teaching Resources

Project Notes: Conducting Oral History in the Secondary Classroom, by Kerry McKibbin

This curriculum guide (Student Press Initiative, 2005) provides a detailed narrative, framework, and student examples for creating an oral history curriculum and publishing program in your classroom.
http://www.lulu.com/content/1354197

Studs Terkel's Working: A Teaching Guide, by Rick Ayers

An invaluable educational resource (The New Press, 2001) for introducing Studs Terkel's classic work of oral history to today's students.
http://www.amazon.com/Studs-Terkels-Working-Rick-Ayers/dp/1565846265

Like It Was: A Complete Guide to Writing Oral History, by Cynthia Stokes Brown

In this how-to guide (Teachers & Writers Collaborative, 1988) Brown succeeds in sharing her oral history methods with prospective historians. Separate chapters focus on using the tape recorder, interview techniques, transcription of the interview, editing, writing short pieces or full biographies, and publishing the results.
http://www.amazon.com/Like-Was-Complete-Writing-History/dp/0915924129

Oral History: An Introduction for Students, by James Hoopes

A how-to oral history manual (University of North Carolina Press, 1979) designed especially for students.
http://www.amazon.com/Oral-History-Introduction-James-Hoopes/dp/0807813443

Doing Oral History: A Practical Guide (2nd edition), by Donald A. Ritchie

This comprehensive handbook (Oxford University Press, 2003) explains the principles and guidelines created by the Oral History Association to ensure the professional standards of oral historians.
http://www.amazon.com/Doing-Oral-History-Donald-Ritchie/dp/0195154347/

The Oral History Manual (American Association for State and Local History Book Series), by Barbara W. Sommer and Mary Kay Quinlan

This manual (AltaMira Press, 2003) offers step-by-step instructions, checklists, full-size reproducible forms, project descriptions and summary sheets, and extensive illustrations to help guide readers in taking ideas for an oral history project and turning them into a successful format.
http://www.amazon.com/History-Manual-American-Association-State/dp/0759101019/

Dialogue with the Past: Engaging Students and Meeting Standards through Oral History, by Glenn Whitman

Tips, examples from students and teachers, and reproducible forms, along with an comprehensive bibliography, make this book (AltaMira Press, 2004) a vital tool for anyone working with secondary students to plan and carryout oral history projects.
http://www.amazon.com/Dialogue-Past-Engaging-Standards-Association/dp/0759106495/

Websites

Studs Terkel in the Classroom

This website from the Chicago Historical Society provides a host of educational tools and documents for students, teachers and the general public, including sample lesson plans on oral history with suggestions for how to use Studs Terkel recordings in the classroom.
http://www.studsterkel.org/education.php

Institute for Oral History at Baylor University

This site offers an "Oral History Workshop on the Web" which includes an overview, guidance for K-12 teachers and students in planning and executing oral history research, transcribing style guide, interview tips and more.
http://www.baylor.edu/Oral_History/

Oral History Association

The website of the Oral History Association, founded in 1966, features an educators section which includes an overview on how to use oral history in your classroom; post-secondary and professional oral history programs and projects; a list of pre-collegiate oral history projects; and, a directory of nationwide oral history educator workshops.
http://alpha.dickinson.edu/oha/org_com_ed_test.html

StoryCorps

A modern oral history project supported by National Public Radio, StoryCorps sets up booths with audio recording equipment in cities across America. The result: a national sound portrait of modern America.
www.storycorps.net

Folklore Project

In 1936, the U.S. government paid more than 300 writers from 24 states to travel around the country and document the oral histories of thousands of Americans. These oral histories are preserved in the Library of Congress and online.
www.memory.loc.gov/ammem/wpaintro

FamilySearch

In a vault built into a mountain in Utah, the Church of Jesus Christ of Latter-day Saints (Mormons) holds the world's largest family history collection, including oral histories, genealogical charts, and records from all over the world.
www.familysearch.com

Go Deeper: **Additional Resources**

If you are interested in developing a classroom unit or workshop on the larger themes covered in *This is Where I Need to Be*, the following books, reports, and websites can serve as valuable resources.

Teaching Resources

Saudi Aramco World Magazine
This indispensable publication, and its companion website, offers a wealth of expert knowledge on Muslim art, architecture, culture, history and heritage. Subscriptions to the magazine are free, as is a DVD compilation of all its magazines complete with photos, bibliography and more.
http://www.saudiaramcoworld.com/issue/200805/

Being Muslim, by Haroon Siddiqui, Groundwood Books, 2008
This guide is intended to provide high school and college students with comprehensive, informed answers to historical and current events—both national and international—connected to Muslims.
http://www.amazon.com/Muslim-Groundwork-Guides-Haroon-Siddiqui/dp/0888998872

Muslim Holidays: Teacher's Guide and Student Resources, by Susan L. Douglass, Council on Islamic Education, 2006
A guide to better acquaint both teachers and students with Muslim holidays.
http://www.amazon.com/Muslim-Holidays-Teachers-Student-Resources/dp/1930109075

Timeline of Islam
A Brief Timeline of Events in the History of Islam.
http://www.pbs.org/wgbh/pages/frontline/teach/muslims/timeline.html

A Glossary of Islamic Terms
Terms that are used often in the discussion of Islam and Muslims.
http://www.pbs.org/wgbh/pages/frontline/teach/muslims/glossary.html

Islam
An overview of Islam, with links to resources, from the Religion Newswriters Association.
http://www.rnasecure.org/guide/islam.html

When Hate Hits Home
A guide to talking to kids about terrorism, from the award winning publication Teaching Tolerance.
http://www.tolerance.org/news/article_tol.jsp?id=272

Research Studies & Reports: U.S. Religious Landscape Survey
Based on interviews with more than 35,000 American adults, this extensive survey by the Pew Forum on Religion & Public Life details the religious makeup, religious beliefs and practices as well as social and political attitudes of the American public, including the Muslim community.
http://religions.pewforum.org/

Who Speaks for Islam? What A Billion Muslims Really Think, by John Esposito and Dalia Mogahed, Gallup Press, 2008
Based on six years of research by the Gallup Organization and 50,000 plus interviews with Muslims in more than 35 nations with predominantly or sizable Muslim populations. Teaching Guide available.
http://www.amazon.com/Who-Speaks-Islam-Billion-Muslims/dp/1595620176

Muslims in Metropolis, by Kavitha Rajagopalan, Rutgers University Press, 2008
A thorough and insightful examination of the identity formation and experiences of three very different Muslim families in the West—in London, New York, and Berlin. This is a good read for college and adult audiences, but excerpts would work in the classroom as well because of the author's journalistic style.
http://www.amazon.com/Muslims-Metropolis-Stories-Immigrant-Families/dp/0813543444

American Muslim Voter Survey
A Survey by the Council on American-Islamic Relations details how many Muslim Voters there were in 2006 and related demographics.
http://www.cair.com/Portals/0/pdf/American_Muslim_Voter_Survey_2006.pdf

Muslims in America: Profile 2001, by Abdul Malik Mujahid
An annotated resource listing data on the number of Muslims in the USA.
http://www.soundvision.com/info/yearinreview/2001/profile.asp

Washington Report on Middle East Affairs
A trusted source on America and its relations in the Middle East covering politics and current affairs. It is published by the American Educational Trust (AET)
http://www.washington-report.org/

News

Muslims in America: Coverage, by Andrea Elliot
Series of stories, interactive segments, audio and photos by New York Times journalist Andrea Elliot who won a Pulitzer for her reporting on Muslims in America.
http://topics.nytimes.com/top/news/national/series/muslimsinamerica/index.html

Muslim Comedian Aims at Breaking Stereotypes
Dean Obeidallah, an Arab American comedian, talks to National Public Radio about how he's using his comedy to break stereotypes about Muslims and Arabs in America.
http://www.npr.org/templates/story/story.php?storyId=11746247

Haroon Siddiqui, Toronto Star Editor & Columnist
Award winning author, Haroon Siddiqui, writes on issues pertaining to national and international current events, and local and international politics, with extensive writings on Muslims.
http://www.thestar.com/comment/columnists/94618

"The Reason We Haven't Heard American Muslims Condemning Terrorism," by Paul Barrett
The author argues that Muslims have spoken out against terrorism, but just not the way Americans are likely to hear it.
http://www.salon.com/opinion/feature/2007/03/01/barrett/

"The Only Acceptable Form of Racism Left: Islamophobia," by Abdul Malik Mujahid
The writer illustrates the many ways Islam and Muslims have become "dirty words".
http://www.soundvision.com/info/racism/islamophobia.asp

Powell Endorses Obama for President
Former Secretary of State, Colin Powell, criticizes American public, politicians and media on turning Islam and Muslims into negatives.
http://www.msnbc.msn.com/id/27265369/

Carnegie Council – The Voice for Ethics in International Policy
Transcript of a talk by journalist Paul Barrett, author of American Islam: Struggle for the Soul of a Religion, where he explores the complexity of the over six million Muslims of different backgrounds who live in the United States.
http://www.cceia.org/resources/transcripts/5423.html

Interactive & Educational Websites

The Islam Project
Muslim teens speak out as part of a multimedia effort, using print and video in schools and communities, to facilitate an understanding of Islam, Muslims and the American Muslim. A Facilitators Guide is available.
http://www.islamproject.org/

Simulated Hajj from PBS' Muhammad: Legacy of a Prophet
Students can participate in a simulated Hajj, the annual pilgrimage to Mecca that Muslims are urged to perform once in a lifetime.
http://www.pbs.org/muhammad/virtualhajj.shtml

Bridge-Builders
A website for youth to share their experiences related to inter-faith service learning opportunities, gain insights on current happenings in inter-faith work, and more.
http://bridge-builders.ning.com/

Change the Story
An online resource aimed at transforming harmful stereotypes about Muslims that persist in society.
http://changethestory.net/

Listen Up
An organization that teaches students to use film and video as a platform to express themselves. Completed works are screened at International Film Festivals and on Public TV.
www.listenup.org

Picture Books

The White Nights of Ramadan, by Maha Addasi, Boyds mill Press, 2008
An uncommon story about a festival known as Girgian that comes in the middle of the holy month of Ramadan, and is celebrated in nations by the Persian Gulf.
http://www.amazon.com/White-Nights-Ramadan-Maha-Addasi/dp/1590785231

One Green Apple, by Eve Bunting, Clarion Books, 2006
A sensitive tale of a contemporary Arab immigrant child who is learning to fit in.
http://www.amazon.com/One-Green-Apple-Eve-Bunting/dp/0618434771

I Don't Want to Blow You Up, by Ricardo Cortes and Bowman Hastie Magic Propaganda Mill Books, 2007
A coloring book that aims to counter the frightening messages bandied in the name of the "War on Terror" by drawing attention to the myriad people of different colors and cultures who are living peaceful and meaningful lives. A free educator's guide available online at www.blowyouup.com/edu.
http://www.blowyouup.com/

The Last Night of Ramadan, by Maissa Hamed, Bell Pond Books, 2007
Explores the traditions of the Muslim holy month of Ramadan.
http://www.amazon.com/Last-Night-Ramadan-Maissa-Hamed/dp/0880105860

The Color of Home, by Mary Hoffman, Dial Press, 2002
An African refugee Muslim child finds a way to fill his pictures with color, despite the horrific images that haunt him.
http://www.amazon.com/Color-Home-Mary-Hoffman/dp/0803728417

The Night of the Moon: A Muslim Holiday Story, by Hena Khan, Chronicle Books, 2008
The author shares how one Muslim American family celebrates Ramadan and Eid.
http://www.amazon.com/Night-Moon-Muslim-Holiday-Story/dp/0811860620

My Name Was Hussein, by Hristo Kyuchukov, Boyds Mill Press, 2004
Traces the experiences of a young Roma boy who lives in Bulgaria. Hussein introduces readers to the blend of many cultures and traditions that his family has incorporated over the centuries.
http://www.amazon.com/Name-Was-Hussein-Hristo-Kyuchukov/dp/1563979640

Silent Music, by James Rumford, Roaring Brook Press, 2008
A child protagonist shares the harshness of war in Baghdad even as he expresses himself via the beauty and discipline of Arabic calligraphy.
http://www.amazon.com/Silent-Music-James-Rumford/dp/1596432764

My Name Is Bilal, by Asma Mobin Uddin, Boyds Mill Press, 2005
When Bilal and his sister transfer to a school where they are the only Muslims, they must learn how to fit in while staying true to their beliefs and heritage.
http://www.amazon.com/My-Name-Bilal-Asma-Mobin-Uddin/dp/1590781759

The Librarian of Basra: A True Story From Iraq By Jeanette Winter, Harcourt Childrens Books, 2005

This story re-counts the efforts made by a librarian in Basra, Iraq to save her precious library, including an ancient copy of the Quran—the holy book of Muslims—from destruction.
http://www.amazon.com/Librarian-Basra-True-Story-Iraq/dp/0152054456

Fiction

Does My Head Look Big in This, by Randa Abdel-Fattah, Scholastic, 2008

When 16-year-old Amal makes the decision to start wearing the hijab fulltime, everyone has a reaction.
http://www.amazon.com/Does-Head-Look-Big-This/dp/043992233X

Ask Me No Questions, by Marina Budhos, Simon Pulse, 2007

A Bangladeshi family is split up after 9/11 when the father is detained for not having a valid passport.
http://www.amazon.com/Ask-Me-Questions-Marina-Budhos/dp/1416949208

Memoirs

The Other Side of the Sky, by Farah Ahmedi, Simon Spotlight Entertainment, 2006

In this memoir, an Afghani Muslim refugee girl discovers herself and an American woman whom she calls her second mother in this book on holding onto the identity one is born with, and the pains of forging a new one in your adopted homeland.
http://www.amazon.com/Other-Side-Sky-Memoir/dp/141691837X

The Language of Baklava, by Diana Abu-Jaber, Anchor, 2006

In this memoir, a Jordanian-American Muslim girl straddles her Jordanian heritage and her American mother's culture and shares her experiences on being a multi-hyphenated girl then woman.
http://www.amazon.com/Abu-Jaber-Diana-language-baklava-memoir/dp/B000IZJWD8

Persepolis, by Marjane Satrapi, Pantheon, 2004

A graphic memoir about growing up as a girl in revolutionary Iran.
http://www.amazon.com/Persepolis-Story-Childhood-Marjane-Satrapi/dp/037571457X

In the Shadow of No Towers, by Art Spiegelman, Viking, 2004

The Pulitzer Prize-winning graphic artist reflects on his 9/11 experience and the ways in which life changed thereafter.
http://www.amazon.com/Shadow-No-Towers-Art-Spiegelman/dp/0670915416

Three Cups of Tea, by Greg Mortenson, Puffin, 2009

A young reader's edition of the worldwide bestseller Three Cups of Tea, this book follows mountaineer Greg Mortenson on his journey to becoming a humanitarian by promoting peace one school at a time in the rugged mountains of Pakistan.
http://www.amazon.com/Three-Cups-Tea-Journey-World/dp/0142414123/

Acts of Faith: The Story of an American Muslim, the Struggle for the Soul of a Generation, by Eboo Patel

A Muslim youngster struggles to forge his identity as a Muslim, an Indian and an American.
http://www.amazon.com/Acts-Faith-American-Struggle-Generation/dp/sitb-next/0807077267

Films

One Nation, Many Voices Contest

Winners of a documentary contest inviting submissions on the theme "Muslims in America: Stories, Not Stereotypes." This contest was sponsored by Link TV.
http://www.linktv.org/onenation

Through the Eyes of Immigrants

This 23-minute Educational Video Center documentary has a particular emphasis on Arab and Muslim teenagers and how they have been stereotyped and discriminated against after 9/11.
http://www.mediarights.org/film/through_the_eyes_of_immigrants.php

PBS' Cities of Light: The Rise and Fall of Islamic Spain

This documentary tells the story of a time when Muslims, Christians, and Jews co-existed in unparalleled harmony, and built a society that was to spark the Renaissance. A Teacher's Guide is available.
http://www.pbs.org/citiesoflight/

PBS' Muhammad: The Legacy of a Prophet

A documentary showcasing the life and experiences of the Prophet of Islam, Muhammad.
http://www.pbs.org/muhammad/

PBS' Islam: Empire of Faith
A look at the history of the Islamic World over 1000 years and large expanses of the world. Teachers Resources available.
http://www.pbs.org/empires/islam/

Beyond Borders: Personal Stories from a Small Planet
A Listen Up! Series of short documentaries by youth focusing on their fears and building security including pieces by Muslims in Amaan and the USA.
http://www.listenup.org/projects/beyondborders/

Frontline: Muslims
Frontline, through interviews, its documentaries and website, examines the role that Islam plays in different lives, including in Muslim America.
http://www.pbs.org/wgbh/pages/frontline/shows/muslims/

Allah Made Me Funny
Fighting stereotypes with humor, this film and standup comedy routine lifts the veil on identity and what it means to be Muslim in America.
http://www.allahmademefunny.com/

Arranged
A film that explores questions of identity and friendship between a Orthodox Jewish woman and a conservative Muslim woman in America.
http://www.arrangedthemovie.com/

The Visitor
A film that examines the ties that bind across boundaries of race and religion, in the context of illegal immigration in the USA. Rated PG-13.
http://www.thevisitorfilm.com/

Magazines

Emel Magazine
A "Muslim lifestyle magazine" with subscribers worldwide, sold in mainstream bookstores in Britain.
http://www.emelmagazine.com/

Islamic Horizons
A publication of the Islamic Society of North America, a window to the lives of Muslim Americans, touching on current events and spirituality.
http://www.isna.net/Islamic-Horizons/pages/Islamic-Horizons.aspx

Islamica Magazine
Islamica Magazine offers an enlightened, global perspective on Islam and a platform for Muslim intellectual voices.
http://www.islamicamagazine.com/

Muslim Girl Magazine
A Muslim girl's alternative to Cosmopolitan and Seventeen, with a dash of spirituality.
http://www.muslimgirlworld.com/

Q News – The Muslim Magazine
Based in Britain, this glossy covers spirituality, current affairs and culture.
http://www.q-news.com/

America's Muslim Family Magazine
America's leading magazine that focuses on raising a Muslim family with Islamic values, amidst everyday challenges.
http://www.americasmuslimfamily.com

Educational Organizations

Islamic Networks Group (ING)
ING is an educational organization in San Francisco that delivers presentations relating to Islam and the Muslim world with the goal of eliminating stereotyping through education. Teachers interested in inviting religious leaders or scholars into the classroom can find contact information on this website:
http://www.ing.org/about_us.htm

Organization of Islamic Speakers Midwest (OISM)
Chicago based speakers offer presentations on Islam 101 at schools, civic centers and community organizations including police stations, fire stations and chambers of commerce.
http://www.oismidwest.org/

The Council on Islamic Education
A resource for educators and students to facilitate the discussion of religion, specifically Islam, in the classroom. Teachers can invite religious leaders or scholars to make classroom presentations.
www.cie.org

Interfaith Youth Corps

A Chicago-based interfaith organization founded by Eboo Patel dedicated to promoting mutual respect and religious pluralism through leadership training and collaborative community service projects.

We the Poets

A Philadelphia-based organization that brings school children from different cultures and faiths together to write and share poetry.
www.artsandspirituality.org/we_the_poets/

Poetry Pals

A Chicago-based organization that brings school children from different cultures and faiths together to write and share poetry.
www.poetrypals.org

Changing Worlds

A Chicago-based educational nonprofit arts organization which works with schools and communities to promote cross-cultural understanding through the arts, oral history, and literacy.
www.changingworlds.org